Advance Praise for
Wall Street Research: Past, Present, and Future

"Professors Groysberg and Healy are two of world's foremost authorities on Wall Street research. This book is a must-read for anyone interested in the state of investment research and its future. It examines the industry with thorough academic research and interviews with industry insiders to provide important insights on the role of Wall Street research in capital markets."
—**Barry Hurewitz,** Managing Director and Chief Operating Officer, Morgan Stanley Investment Research

"Groysberg and Healy bring alive the evolution of equity research over the past fifty years through bull and bear markets. Their analysis of key factors, such as independence of research and measurements of performance, provides a blueprint for the future of equity research as an engine for generating value for investors."
—**Stefano Natella,** Managing Director and Global Head of Research, Credit Suisse

"As a manager of buy-side analysts, this book is invaluable to my work. The buy-side is naturally opaque and issues related to compensation, team structure, and performance can be difficult to benchmark with competitors. We often ask ourselves how many stocks an analyst can reasonably cover and how to best leverage sell-side research. The findings in *Wall Street Research* provide important clues about how the industry can manage these questions. I have not seen anything like it."
—**Guillermo R. Araoz,** Former Director of Equities, Morgan Asset Management

"Groysberg and Healy are the preeminent chroniclers of Wall Street, having amassed an unsurpassed treasure trove of history and knowledge from their decades-long pursuit of the personalities, institutions, and regulations that have made the industry what it is today. *Wall Street Research* explores potential business models and platforms for the continuing evolution of sell-side research. The importance of independent research for our industry, for the economy, and for individual investors makes this a must-read."
—**Jay C. Plourde,** Executive Director, CLSA Americas

"Full of institutional details that deepen our understanding of sell-side research, this book provides penetrating insights into the role that financial analysts play in stock markets."
—**Patricia Dechow,** UC Berkeley

"In one short volume, the authors provide a historic perspective on Wall Street research, while offering crisp and insightful views on topics that can seem intangible and amorphous, even to those who are steeped in the traditions of the business. The book is a valuable resource for experienced analysts, investors, brokers, and regulators; it is also a great read for those who are about to embark on a career in research, and for those of us who are getting ready to look back on one."
—**Stephen J. Buell,** Director of US Equity Research, Canaccord Genuity Inc.

"An important objective analysis that should be read by all who want to understand the role and value of analysts. It should be mandatory reading for researchers, journalists, and regulators who deal with these professionals. "
—**Trevor S. Harris,** Columbia University and Former Managing Director and Vice Chairman, Morgan Stanley

"*Wall Street Research: Past, Present, and Future* provides the reader with an excellent historical perspective on sell-side research. Groysberg and Healy clearly describe the many challenges that research departments have faced over the years, and take an insightful look at what firms have done to overcome those obstacles. They do a fabulous job of painting the picture of an ever-evolving business model."
—**Tom Maloney,** Managing Director and Director of Research, Needham & Company

"As an analyst and research director for more than 30 years, I can say that the authors did an outstanding job of describing the analyst role and the increasingly difficult challenges presented by technology and regulatory change."
—**Robert P. Anastasi,** Senior Managing Director and Director of Equity Research, Raymond James & Associates

"A great read for people interested in the nitty-gritty of sell-side research trends. I especially liked the analysis of the particular responses from the sell-side to different realities in the ever-changing economics of the business."
—**Andres Ramon Cuellar Davila,** Head of Equity Research Sales LATAM, GBM

"High quality investment research is critical for the efficient operation of any capital market. This is one way in which investment banks can unequivocally deliver constructive input as they redefine their role in society after the global financial crisis. However, as the authors deftly highlight, the business model for funding research has long been a challenging and rapidly evolving puzzle, making this book a compelling read for anyone interested in the evolution of financial markets."
—**Damien Horth,** Managing Director and Head of Research, Asia and Japan, UBS AG

"Filled with rich data, *Wall Street Research* gives us a new understanding of the role of equity research in the financial services industry. It should be a go-to source for anyone who wants to learn about where equity research has been, how it has responded to important challenges and opportunities, and where it's likely headed in the future."
—**Mark Chen,** Georgia State University

"To most individual investors, sell-side analysts are in a 'black box.' And yet, they play a key role. This comprehensive and lucid examination of the responsibilities, incentives, compensation, performance, and the history of sell-side analysts delivers a powerful and much-needed introduction to the role that they play as market intermediaries."
—**Yingmei Cheng,** Florida State University

Wall Street Research

Wall Street Research

Past, Present, and Future

Boris Groysberg and Paul M. Healy

STANFORD ECONOMICS AND FINANCE
An Imprint of Stanford University Press
Stanford, California

Stanford University Press
Stanford, California

Special discounts for bulk quantities of titles in the Stanford Economics and Finance imprint are
available to corporations, professional associations, and other organizations. For details and
discount information, contact the special sales department of Stanford University Press.
Tel: (650) 736-1782, Fax: (650) 736-1784

Printed in the United States of America on acid-free, archival-quality paper

Library of Congress Cataloging-in-Publication Data
Groysberg, Boris, author.
    Wall Street research : past, present, and future / Boris Groysberg and Paul M. Healy.
    pages cm
    Includes bibliographical references and index.
    ISBN 978-0-8047-8531-0 (cloth : alk. paper)
    1. Investment analysis—United States. 2. Investment advisors—United States. 3. Stocks—
Research—United States. 4. Securities industry—United States. I. Healy, Paul M., author.
II. Title.
    HG4529.G76 2013
    332.63'2042—dc23
                                                                            2013011216

ISBN 978-0-8047-8712-3 (electronic)

Typeset by Thompson Type in 11/14 Bembo Standard

Dedicated to our families for all their support.

Contents

Preface

Wall Street or sell-side equity analysts provide research products and services on publicly traded companies to institutional and retail investors (collectively referred to as the "buy side") to help them make more profitable investment decisions. In supplying this research, sell-side analysts also provide a service to the companies they analyze by helping to create a liquid market for their stocks. As a result of their role as financial intermediaries that serve two distinct constituencies, each with its own agenda, sell-side analysts face inherent conflicts of interest.

During the last ten years the sell-side industry has been battered by a series of shocks. As concerns over conflicts of interest mounted, the integrity of its research output was questioned, leading to transformative regulatory changes. New technologies emerged to democratize information and change the way stocks are traded, threatening the industry's product and business model. There were upheavals and stagnation in established core financial markets such as the United States, Japan, and Western Europe. And burgeoning new markets in countries such as China and India raised potential challenges to the dominance of leading firms.

Despite our common interest in the sell-side equity industry and in these changes, our areas of expertise are quite different. Boris's prior research examines how financial intermediaries acquire, develop, and reward star sell-side analysts, whereas Paul's focuses on the tools that enable sell-side analysts to develop insights into firms' competitive positioning and to assess their values. Yet our fascination with the changes we have lived through during the last ten years brought us together to write this book.

Actually, we didn't start out to write a book. Instead, over time we undertook a series of case studies, field interviews, and academic studies that we hoped would provide us with insights into the effects of the above changes and the industry's future.[1] But as we reflected on the portfolio of research we had completed, we recognized that it told a fascinating story of an industry that has proven to be remarkably resilient in resolving economic and regulatory challenges. Our goal is to provide practitioners and academics with a deeper understanding of the forces that have shaped the industry and the factors that account for its resilience.

The book consists of eight chapters. Chapter 1, "The Rise and Fall of Equity Research at Prudential," profiles how the Prudential Insurance Company built and dismantled a research department over almost three decades. The Prudential story highlights many of the key trends that have affected sell-side research over time, focusing on, among other things, the financial pressures faced by sell-side research departments due to the delinking of investment banking and research and the move to low-cost trading platforms resulting in lower per share commissions.

In Chapter 2, "What Do Analysts Do, and How Are They Managed?," we look closely at the job of an equity research analyst: what they do, how they are hired, how they are evaluated, and how they are compensated. Chapter 3, "Sell-Side Research: The History of an Information Good," reviews the economic challenges that sell-side firms experience in monetizing their research output and discusses the two models that have been developed to mitigate problems of information goods and generate revenues for sell-side research, the trading commission model and the investment banking model.

In Chapter 4, "Investment Banking Model Challenges," we examine the rise of the investment banking model in the 1990s and the impact that it had on the sell-side industry. We evaluate the impact of the Global Settlement of 2003 on the use of investment banking to fund research.

Chapter 5, "Challenges to Trading Commission Model," explores the recent evolution of the trading commission model and the challenges that this model has faced due to the enactment of Regulation Fair Disclosure (Reg FD) in 2000 and to technological advancements that have had an impact on stock trading as well as information gathering and dissemination.

Chapter 6, "The Performance of Sell-Side Research Analysts Revisited," presents our findings on sell-side analysts' performance by comparing quantitative measures of analyst performance for different types of sell-side analysts, such as those at investment banks and those at brokerage firms. We then examine how sell-side analysts' performance compares to that of their buy-side counterparts.

Chapter 7, "The Future of Sell-Side Research in the United States," examines a variety of innovations by sell-side research firms in the United States in response to the regulatory and technology challenges discussed in Chapters 4 and 5. Many of these innovations seek to segment the research market and provide firms with opportunities to provide more valued services to their leading clients.

Chapter 8, "Sell-Side Research in Emerging Markets," looks at the development of the sell-side research industry in China and India. We discuss the factors that have enabled sell-side research in these countries to enjoy rapid growth and more attractive pricing than in the United States.

Finally, in Chapter 9, we draw conclusions about the industry, its challenges, and its future.

Acknowledgments

There are many people at Harvard Business School, in the financial industry, and in our lives who have contributed in one way or another to this book and to whom we would like to express our sincere thanks. Some offered great insights or access to proprietary data, while others offered babysitting services. We are deeply indebted to the individuals and institutions in the financial industry that contributed to the content of this book and provided meaningful insight by granting access to information and participating in research interviews.

We are grateful to Sarah Abbott for her help in collecting the company and interview data that have been used throughout the book, as well as her partnership in writing cases on this topic. We are also grateful to Geoff Marietta for conducting background research, interviews, and analysis. His efforts, including the acquisition of hard-to-find data, helped shape several sections of this book.

We appreciate the comments of the following people: Steve Balog, Steve Buell, our editor Margo Beth Fleming, Fred Fraenkel, Chris Marquis, Karthik Ramanna, Jack Rivkin, George Serafeim, and two reviewers of an earlier manuscript. In addition, we have had many conversations with colleagues at Harvard Business School about this book, and we are grateful for their advice and suggestions. We would like to thank Hitesh Zaver for his data on emerging markets and Sophie Hood for her research support. Lisa Paige's assistance in editing has been invaluable. We thank Kate Connolly for her efforts in coordinating with the publisher.

We thank our coauthors on the various projects we have undertaken in this area and whose joint research work with us is discussed throughout the book. These include Amanda Cowen, Craig Chapman, Grace Gui, David Maber, Nitin Nohria, George Serafeim, and Devin Shanthikumar.

Financial support for our research has been generously provided by the Division of Research and Faculty Development at Harvard Business School.

Finally, we thank our families for their patience and support of our work.

Wall Street Research

1

The Rise and Fall of Equity Research at Prudential

In the span of twenty-six years, the insurance giant Prudential entered and then exited the stock brokerage industry. Prudential's story illustrates many of the changes and challenges facing the equity research industry during this period. Like many competitors, Prudential entered the industry as part of a "financial supermarket" strategy. Lured by attractive fees, Prudential subsequently built an investment banking business leveraged through equity research. The firm was also among the first to recognize the conflicts of interest between equity research and banking, and voluntarily closed its investment banking business prior to regulatory changes created to mitigate such conflicts. The resulting business model focused on providing investors with trustworthy investment advice and trade execution. However, this model was tested by sharp declines in trading commissions brought about by electronic trading. As a result, despite having a highly ranked equity research department, Prudential exited the industry in June 2007.

Material included in Chapter 1, including all the quotes of the senior managers and analysts, is derived largely from the Harvard Business School case: Boris Groysberg, Paul M. Healy, and Amanda Cowen, "Prudential Securities," HBS No. 104-008 (Boston: Harvard Business School Publishing, 2004). Reprinted by permission of Harvard Business School. Copyright © 2004 by the President and Fellows of Harvard College.

Insurance History

Prudential Insurance Company was founded by John Dryden in 1875 to provide life insurance to working-class families. The company was named after Prudential Assurance Company of Great Britain, a pioneer in industrial insurance on the other side of the Atlantic. The company quickly developed a reputation for financial stability, inspiring the well-recognized symbol "The Rock."

During the 1970s, Donald MacNaughton, Prudential's chief executive officer (CEO), encouraged employees to think of Prudential's business as selling, not just providing, insurance. This approach led Prudential to expand into auto and homeowners' insurance. MacNaughton believed that Prudential's continued prosperity could be assured only by leveraging the firm's selling capabilities and finding new ways to serve policyholders.[1] Insurance was certainly one component of a customer's financial needs, but there were many others. MacNaughton and his successors worried that unless Prudential could broaden its product offerings, other financial services firms could capture a portion of their customer base by offering a broad array of financial services through a single distribution network.

The Acquisition of the Bache Group Inc.

In early 1981, the Bache Group was looking for help. For two years, management had been trying to fend off a hostile takeover attempt by First City Financial, a Canadian financial services company owned by the Belzberg family. The family had acquired more than 20 percent of the company despite defensive maneuvers by Bache management, and most insiders considered the takeover virtually inevitable.[2] However, Bache's CEO, Harry Jacobs, had one last plan—in February 1981 he launched a search for another potential acquirer.

Garnett Keith, a senior vice president, was the first person at Prudential to be contacted about acquiring Bache. Keith reported, "I received a phone call from Bob Baylis at First Boston, and he asked me if Prudential would like to acquire Bache. And I said well, not likely, but let me talk to the chairman. So I went and talked to Bob Beck, and he thought about it and was quite enthusiastic."

At the time, Bache was primarily a retail brokerage firm serving individual customers, although not a very prestigious one. An analyst recruited to the firm recalled his first weeks on the job:

Bache was headquartered at 100 Gold Street, which was one of the seediest, most disgusting buildings in Manhattan. The furniture looked awful, and the orange carpeting was worn down to its last few threads. It was not a place to which you'd want to bring anyone you were trying to impress. Bache had a poor reputation among institutional investors, and it had no investment banking that anyone could see. It did have a large retail sales force, but it often seemed in bad spirits, was not terribly successful, and was not well respected. During my first few months at Bache I recall moments when I found myself staring at my rotary-dial telephone and feeling as if I was back in the nineteenth century.

Despite Bache's marginal position in the industry, Beck saw the acquisition as a way to jump-start Prudential's "financial supermarket" strategy. The goal was to turn Prudential into a one-stop shop for all of a customer's financial service needs. Beck understood that the quality of Bache's products (especially its equity research) would have to be improved, but he also envisioned a day when insurance agents would sell mutual funds and brokers would sell life insurance. Keith explained why Beck was so confident that Prudential could effectively harness these synergies:

> Bob Beck was a consummate marketing executive. He had run Prudential's agency organization and was very confident in his ability to manage people selling products on commission. What he saw in Bache was another commission-driven sales organization that additional products could be put through. At the time, Bache clearly had mediocre products and therefore was not able to attract and hold top talent. Beck felt that Prudential could upgrade Bache's product and then could attract and hold a better quality of financial advisors, which is what really drives business.

Others, like Fred Fraenkel, a former research director at the firm, were more skeptical and harbored doubts as to whether Prudential understood the complexities of the stock brokerage industry. He explained:

> Prudential was a really large mutual insurance company that had tens of millions of lives insured. It was based in Newark and run by insurance company executives whose motto was "perpetual and invulnerable." That had little to do with returns or profitability or cost or policyholders. "You give me money, you're going to die, I'm going to pay your policy face amount." What assures that? That we're perpetual and invulnerable. So they had a view of the world that didn't really have anything to do with what went on in the rest of the financial services continuum.

In March 1981, Prudential Insurance Company of America offered $385 million to acquire Bache Group Inc. The deal was consummated the following year. Although Bache had a small investment banking operation, there were no plans to grow that business. Keith explained why:

> The investment side of the Prudential organization was quite concerned that if we owned something that had even a fledgling investment banking operation, it was going to foul up our relationships with the bulge-bracket (most prestigious) investment banks that were necessary to keep our cash flow invested. Through the whole acquisition process, less was more. Less investment banking made it more attractive to Prudential. The last thing we wanted was investment banking activity over at Bache that could potentially ruin a much more important cash investment process at Prudential, the parent. Investment banking was a concern, not an attraction.

New Management at Bache

Shortly after the acquisition, Prudential began looking for someone to lead the new company, renamed Prudential-Bache Securities, or Pru-Bache for short. In 1983, George Ball was hired. At the time, Ball was second-in-command at E. F. Hutton, a highly successful retail brokerage firm. Fraenkel described him as an exceptional motivator:

> He was the son of the superintendent of schools of Milburn, New Jersey, a speed reader, a very high-IQ person, a very dynamic person, who had spent his career in a meteoric rise through E. F. Hutton on the retail side of the firm. The thing he was unbelievably good at was personnel management. E. F. Hutton was like Bache, it had several thousand brokers, and he knew every broker's name, and he knew every broker's wife's name, and he knew every kid of every broker and what school they were at. George was a memory-system person; he had "mental compartments" where he could literally memorize thousands of items and recall them instantly. He would ask people personal questions, and everyone felt they were his best friend. He was probably one of the best cheerleader-managers that I've ever been around.

Ball's first priority was to develop the institutional side of the business—to build a research department and a sales and trading organization that could service large institutional investors such as mutual and pension funds. He believed these important capabilities could then be leveraged to develop other businesses. To lead the effort, he looked to his former colleagues. Mike Shea, former president of Prudential's equity group, remembered:

> The first big move was the joining of Greg Smith, Fred Fraenkel, and Ed Yardeni from E. F. Hutton. They came in as the strategy trio. And their mission was to begin the formation of a true institutional business. A lot of institutional salespeople followed from E. F. Hutton and a couple of other places to Pru in the early '80s because they wanted to be involved in the business with them. So that was really the very beginning; that was the genesis.

The "strategy trio" had some success in accomplishing their goals. Pru-Bache began to service institutional clients and started to leverage their new capabilities to better service retail clients as well. Soon the focus turned to investment banking.

Project '89: The Genesis of Investment Banking at Pru-Bache

In the years immediately following the merger, little was done to improve Bache's small investment banking business because of the potential impact on the Prudential Insurance Company's Wall Street relationships. Keith recalled that the decision to expand Pru-Bache's business was undertaken to "internalize some of the investment banking fees that were being paid to the bulge-bracket firms." Prior to May 1, 1975, trading commissions had been regulated, generating fees that covered the costs of trade execution and equity research. However, the May Day deregulation was followed by a steady decline in commissions, reducing the resources available for research.

In 1987 Ball officially launched Project '89, investing close to $200 million over the following two years to attract top new investment banking professionals.[3] The plan was to build one of the best investment banking operations by 1989. Keith, who was present at the executive committee meetings where the project was approved, commented:

> George (Ball) convinced Bob Beck that he should be allowed to build a better investment banking organization. And what he sold Bob Beck

was to be the "best of the rest"—that he knew he'd get his head kicked in if he took on Goldman Sachs, Morgan Stanley, and First Boston, but he needed to be at least as good as PaineWebber. So the franchise and the funding George got from the Prudential board with Bob Beck's blessing was to upgrade Bache's investment banking activity to equal the "best of the rest."

Prior to Project '89, Pru-Bache's investment banking business ranked well behind those of the bulge firms. Furthermore, its current investment banking professionals were not terribly impressive. Therefore, from the outset it was decided that a serious effort to develop investment banking would require new blood. As *Investment Dealer's Digest* put it, ultimately "Project '89 was about hiring, and about spending top dollar to do so."[4] Pru-Bache hired aggressively in all of its divisions: Thirty senior investment bankers joined the firm in the first five months of the project. These professionals were brought in to develop the firm's relationships with Fortune 500 companies in hopes that associations with big companies would translate into large fees and increased visibility.[5]

Pru-Bache recruited most of their new investment bank and research analysts from elite firms, in the hopes of competing against them. The compensation packages offered during Project '89 became legendary. Not only were the salaries and bonuses higher than those paid by many bulge firms, but they were usually guaranteed—not tied to individual or firm performance.[6] A research analyst at a bulge-bracket firm approached by Pru-Bache during Project '89 commented:

> Honestly, they didn't have a lot to offer me. Pru-Bache was a firm with a terrible reputation. It had an investment bank that was in the building stage but had no real presence and no track record. So what they had to offer was, essentially, money. From my perspective, this simply wasn't a big enough incentive to move. At that time, I was an *Institutional Investor–* ranked analyst. The research director at my firm did not want to lose me. When he heard about Prudential's offer, he matched it and I stayed put.

At first, Project '89 appeared to yield positive results (Exhibit 1.1). Prudential-Bache represented Rupert Murdoch in his bid for the *Herald & Weekly* in Australia and completed the Reliance Electric Company management buyout—at the time, one of the largest leveraged buyout divestitures ever done. Its equity underwriting market share rose by over 10 percent,

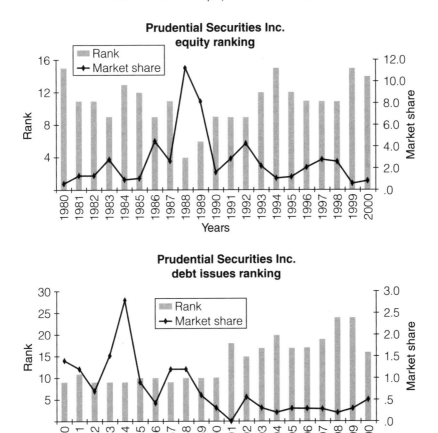

Exhibit 1.1. League tables history: Prudential Securities' market share, 1980–2000.
SOURCE: Thomson Financial DATABASE: U.S. Common Stock (C).

and its ranking shot up from eleventh in 1987 to fourth in 1988. Prudential-Bache's research department also began to move up in the *Institutional Investor* rankings (institutional clients' rankings of research departments). By 1988, it was ranked number five with nearly thirty-five ranked analysts (Exhibit 1.2).

The '87 Crash and the Demise of Project '89

On October 19, 1987, the stock market plummeted, losing more than 20 percent of its value. The crash had a serious impact on all banks, but it hit the fledgling Pru-Bache especially hard. Investment banking deals

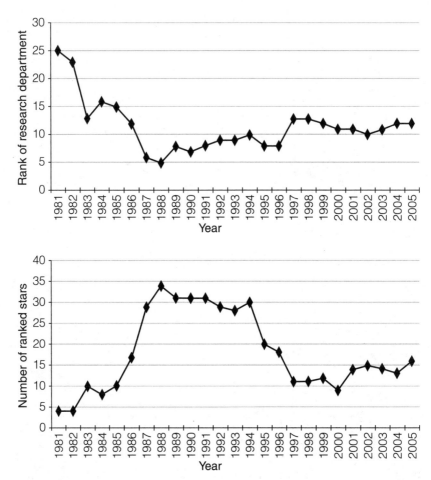

Exhibit 1.2. Performance of Prudential's research department.

NOTE: "Ranked stars" are defined as analysts who receive a "First Team," "Second Team," "Third Team," or "Runner-Up" designation from *Institutional Investor*.

SOURCE: Compiled from *Institutional Investor*, from October 1981 through October 2005.

disappeared, and retail commissions dried up due to falling investor confidence. The following year, Prudential Insurance cut funding for Project '89. Pru-Bache stopped recruiting and let go more than 25 percent of its banking professionals. In 1988, there was a bright spot when the firm completed the Diamandis management buyout of the CBS magazine division. Unfortunately, the market correction of 1989 followed soon after. Pru-Bache posted losses of $50 million in 1989 and $250 million in 1990.[7] In early 1991, George Ball resigned.

There was some controversy over just what caused the project's failure. Clearly the stock market crashes were part of the reason—revenues dried up while Pru-Bache's compensation commitments were fixed. However, some maintained that Prudential Insurance Company effectively killed the project by reneging on its financial commitment before all the necessary personnel were in place.[8] In fact, many pointed to instances in which Prudential failed to support Pru-Bache. Although the insurance company did a great deal of investing, it directed very little of its business to Pru-Bache, preferring instead to deal with the bulge firms. Prudential also limited the types of deals that Pru-Bache could pursue. For example, the firm was not allowed to participate in hostile takeovers, defined by whether "the target company said 'no' at any time during negotiations." This was problematic given that, according to one banker, "target companies routinely said 'no' the first time out as a standard negotiating tactic."[9] Concerning Pru-Bache's relationship with the parent company, Ball commented:

> Prudential was very helpful in terms of providing the appearance of more than adequate capital for any transaction. It was not helpful in terms of cross marketing or relationship sharing. There were a number of restrictions placed upon the investment bank that made it almost impossible for any of the expected synergies to be achieved. In point of fact, I think that people at Prudential went out of their way to drive business outside of the Prudential family, rather than saying that "if you've got equal competence and there are no apparent conflicts, let at least part of the business be done inside." Some people at Prudential Insurance Company would relatively subtly, but nonetheless overtly, give companies a signal that they might be better off using Goldman Sachs or Morgan Stanley than Prudential Securities.

Others involved in Project '89 believed that it was doomed from the start. They argued that the decision to recruit professionals from the bulge-bracket firms was fundamentally flawed because clients ultimately cared about the reputation and track record of the firm, not the banker. Even Ball believed there was some validity to this argument:

> We hired three people to build up the investment banking business in the mid-'80s quite rapidly; hiring people who were managing directors and had very good records at bulge-bracket firms thinking that they could transfer at least some part of their relationship business to Pru-Bache, and that turned out to be a relatively fallacious assumption. The franchise of a

Goldman Sachs or a Morgan Stanley is what made these people outstanding investment banking producers, and torn away from that franchise they could carry relatively little of their business with them. That was my fault for mis-assessing that, or at least letting people move as quickly as they did without testing the premise better.

Keith agreed: "Franchise matters a huge amount in investment banking. The same investment banker may generate a billion dollars in revenue at Goldman Sachs and generate $400 million a year at Prudential-Bache. So you can't afford to match the Goldman Sachs compensation package because he isn't going to generate the revenues to let you pay him."

A comment by Steve Balog, a former Pru-Bache research analyst, also suggested that the timeline for Project '89 was simply too aggressive:

> In order to successfully build an investment bank, you've got to say: This is a 30-year plan. And you know what? All of us that are sitting around here talking about it today, we're all going to be gone. We're going to be gone halfway through, but this is the plan. We're going to establish this institution as a premier player in the industry, but it's going to be beyond us. So if any of us are thinking we're going to be a hero in doing this—forget it! It takes too long—longer than many of us have the tolerance, or patience, or even years left for.

Wick Simmons's Tenure at Prudential Securities

Following Ball's departure, Hardwick "Wick" Simmons was hired as CEO of the recently renamed Prudential Securities. Simmons was a descendant of one of America's oldest banking families. He joined the firm from Shearson, where he was one of the most likable top executives. In fact, many believed that Simmons was selected for the Prudential job precisely because of his affable personality, optimism, and integrity.[10] These characteristics turned out to be quite important because Simmons spent the first few years of his tenure dealing with the fallout from Project '89.

When Simmons arrived at Prudential, morale was low. Prudential Insurance had already fired nearly 75 percent of the investment banking staff and closed other businesses down altogether. Those who remained doubted that the firm could ever become a real player in the industry. There were rumors that Prudential Securities would be sold. One employee remembered: "Every morning we would all come in and open *The*

[*Wall Street*] *Journal* and go to the index to see if Prudential was mentioned or not. We'd hold our breath and pray that it wasn't there. But very often it was and, with few exceptions, the news was bad."

To make matters worse, Prudential Securities faced a barrage of lawsuits and regulatory inquiries over limited partnerships the firm had sold to clients in the late 1980s, ultimately costing $1.4 billion in fines and settlements. Despite these problems, the firm's operations were profitable, and Simmons worked to rebuild its capabilities. He hired and trained professionals from outside the industry, rather than from the bulge firms, and emphasized client service and regulatory compliance. On the investment banking side, Prudential Securities stopped targeting Fortune 500 firms and instead pursued smaller clients in a limited number of industries.

By the late 1990s, with the partnership scandal behind it, Prudential Securities began to have some success. In the first two months of 1996, the firm managed six equity issues that totaled over $400 million. By 1997, Prudential was ranked twelfth in initial public offering market share, and the investment banking division was expected to generate $150 million in revenues. The new strategy seemed to be working. Medium-sized companies, often overlooked by bulge-bracket firms, appreciated the attention and service they received from Prudential Securities. "With Prudential, you always feel like you're their No. 1 client," commented the president of an auto financing firm.[11] The firm was especially successful in the real estate and telecommunications industries and had plans to continue to develop other focal industries, notably consumer goods, energy, specialty finance, health care, and technology. To further this strategy, in 1999, Prudential bought Vector Securities International, Inc., an investment bank that specialized in health care, and Volpe Brown Whelan & Co., a technology investment bank.

Some of Prudential's progress was attributable to the stock market boom of the late 1990s; it was common for second-tier investment banks to gain market share during this time. Nevertheless, Prudential Securities' leadership was hopeful that these gains could be leveraged in the future to help the firm establish a larger presence in the industry.

Exit from Investment Banking

In 2000, Simmons retired, and John Strangfeld, head of the investments division of Prudential Financial, became the new CEO and soon thereafter a vice chairman at Prudential Financial. Only months after Simmons's departure, Strangfeld announced that after nearly twenty years as a full-service investment bank, Prudential Securities would exit the investment banking business and focus exclusively on providing brokerage services to institutional and retail clients. The issue of exiting investment banking had been under consideration at Prudential Financial for some time. Strangfeld explained the decision:

> Our firm had been a survivor for many years but had never really been a winner. We had a strategy that looked like everyone else's, trying to serve both the issuer and the investor, and we had experienced very erratic results. We were faced with three options: carry on with the existing strategy of looking like a smaller-scale version of everyone else, choose a different path, or divest. Our decision was to choose a different path that played to our strengths, and that resulted in a sustainable, differentiated strategy that was better aligned with the needs and aspirations of Prudential Financial. In essence, we decided to cast our lot entirely with the investor. This change eliminated many of the conflicts of interest that you normally see when firms try to serve both the issuer and the investor. It meant we could tell our clients and our employees that Prudential Financial stands for one thing: the investor. All of our energy and resources, as well as every ounce of capital, would be devoted to the investor.

Several factors influenced Strangfeld's decision. First, after years as a mutual company, the Prudential Insurance Company was planning to go public in 2001. To ensure an attractive valuation and a successful offering, it was important to communicate to the financial markets the positioning and fit of all of Prudential's businesses. Strangfeld believed it was important that Prudential Securities adopt a strategy compatible with the goals of the parent company and differentiated from competitors. He believed that some of the company's disappointing performance over the years was attributable to its "me too" strategy. There were also economic reasons to support exiting investment banking at the end of 2000. The markets had started to soften, and Strangfeld knew that a midtier company would find it even more difficult to compete as the demand for investment banking services declined.

The exit decision lay at the heart of a new investor-focused strategy—one Strangfeld believed Prudential Securities was uniquely positioned to pursue. The credibility of research analysts was beginning to be called into question, and Strangfeld thought that a brokerage firm unencumbered by investment banking conflicts would be attractive to investors. Although the firm would continue to serve both institutional and retail clients, Strangfeld believed the new strategy would be especially compelling for retail customers, who had begun to doubt the firm's investment management skills as the value of their portfolios fell. Prudential planned to use its network of more than 4,000 financial advisors as more than just "stock jockeys" plugging the tip of the day. This network would be used to provide financial planning services as well as investment management advice to the retail market.

The new strategy was certainly consistent with that of The Prudential Insurance Company, which had from inception helped individual investors and families plan and invest for the future. It was also a differentiated strategy—without a large sales network it would be difficult for others to follow Prudential's lead profitably. Many of the firms that did have a sizable sales network were deeply entrenched in investment banking (for example, Merrill Lynch); it was unlikely that these firms would choose to exit.

Nevertheless, the new strategy raised several questions. One of the most critical was whether brokerage commissions alone would be sufficient to enable the firm to attract and retain good research analysts, because high-quality research was at the heart of Prudential's new approach. Research departments did not generate any direct revenues—they were cost centers that supported and were funded by other departments in the bank. The new strategy required that Prudential generate commissions through institutional and retail trading to provide funding for research. Would these sources enable Prudential to compete in the market for star analysts? Steve Buell, former director of global equity research, commented:

> We must attract analysts who are investment-oriented, client-focused, highly competitive folks who continually challenge themselves and are bold enough to publish provocative points of view. As a firm, we must stand by these analysts when they are confronted by company executives who are unhappy with their point of view. When the market recovers from its current slump and investment banking activity returns to the Street, our competitors may try to hire our analysts because of their growing success and their enhanced reputation for independence and integrity. It will be our challenge to give these analysts a work environment that offers both independence and a competitive level of compensation.

The exit also raised a question among some industry observers about whether Prudential was exiting the industry too soon. Ironically, the company's decision coincided with the repeal of the Glass-Steagall Act that enabled commercial banks such as Citibank and Chase Manhattan to create financial powerhouses that combined commercial banking, investment banking, and insurance. Given Prudential's experience in combining insurance and investment banking, some considered the firm well placed to grow financial services businesses to compete with the newly formed Citigroup and JPMorgan Chase.

Independent Research Model

Concerns about the timing of Prudential's exit from investment banking subsided as increased evidence of the conflicts of interest between investment banking practices and equity research emerged. In 2001, Elliot Spitzer, attorney general of New York at the time, launched an investigation into the research and underwriting practices of investment banks. The resulting Global Research Analyst Settlement forced the leading investment banks to reduce the interactions between their investment banking and research departments. It appeared that Prudential's new strategy, which centered on providing high-quality and independent research to institutional and retail investors, was perfectly aligned with the new environment. Strangfeld commented:

> In hindsight, discontinuing investment banking was an even better idea than we had realized, because we have experienced a severe economic downturn. To go through this as a 17th ranked investment bank would have been something close to a financial debacle. Our decision became even more appealing as all the conflicts between investment research and underwriting hit the front page. We really feel that we got ahead of the curve, and we stayed there. We have increasing conviction about the wisdom of where we're going. The absence of conflicts in research is clearly a virtue in today's marketplace, and I think our client base respects us for it. The firm also has a differentiated strategy. We have not had the defections of people or the defections of clients that some people thought we would.

Mark Molnar, one of Prudential's institutional salesmen at the time, agreed:

> It looked like we had done a pretty smart thing when we exited because the market ended up falling apart and investment banking was in

a shambles for at least a year or two while we were branding ourselves as a non-investment-bank independent research firm. So we had an initial lift as our client base recognized our independence. Their perception was that they wanted to pay for independent research, and we were a way to do it.

In its nearly twenty years in investment banking, Prudential had achieved only midtier status, controlling less than a 1 percent market share in equity underwritings in 1999 and 2000 (Exhibit 1.1). That, combined with a weakening market and Prudential Insurance Company's desire to go public in 2001 (which subsequently raised $3 billion for the company), made the decision to exit investment banking that much clearer.

Declining Commissions

Between 2000 and 2005, commissions at brokerage firms fell more than 30 percent, from just under six cents per share to four cents; they were predicted to fall to 1.8 cents per share by 2009.[12] Pressure from institutional investors to lower trading costs and the increased use of electronic trading led to the decline. As a result, trading volume conducted through traders declined by 5 percent from February 2005 to February 2006.[13]

Prudential's brokerage business, which lacked a real electronic platform and relied instead on the traditional "high touch" stock trades executed by individual traders, consequently struggled. Mark Molnar remarked on the condition of the trading department at Prudential:

> I think internally and externally trading is widely recognized to be the weakest link. We have to make investments in trading, especially on the electronic trading side. My clients are trying to pay us for the work we did on the research and sales side, but the way we get paid certainly is through trading. And if we're not able to execute properly we're not going to get paid as much.

A salesman in New York added:

> We were generally trading at six cents a share. And then all of a sudden along came electronic trading. I remember going into meetings at money management firms and they said, "Your competitors are coming in for 8/10ths of a penny per share."

The decision to exit investment banking was beginning to come back to haunt Prudential. Jonathon Lang, a former head of Prudential's London office, explained, "The real killer was that the investment banking went up and kept going up, but commission rates kept going down."

Joint Venture with Wachovia

In February of 2003, in a somewhat surprising move, Prudential and Wachovia announced that they would merge their retail brokerage units. The new company became the third largest brokerage firm in the United States, with $537 billion in client assets. Prudential's 4,377 retail brokers joined Wachovia's 8,109, giving the combined firm a national footprint of more than 3,500 brokerage locations.[14] Under the terms of the deal, Wachovia owned 62 percent of the new firm—a joint venture operated as Wachovia Securities—and Prudential owned the remaining 38 percent. At the time, Strangfeld called the two companies a "great fit."[15] He commented:[16]

> There are few opportunities in the marketplace where two firms can join together to build the scale that makes you a major player overnight. We believe we are ideal partners for each other. Our cultures are aligned and both firms are dedicated to putting the client first and offering them the best products and services.

The merger also served another important role for Strangfeld and Prudential: It prevented further losses from the unit. In 2002, Prudential's retail brokerage unit had lost $41 million, and since 2000 more than one-third of its brokers had left.[17] As one Prudential spokesperson said, "A lot of people were urging us to sell, but that was never what we wanted to do. What we wanted to do was find ways to strengthen it and make it more profitable."[18] The deal also included a clause for Prudential to sell its remaining share in the joint venture in two years if things didn't work out.

After the merger, the research analysts, traders, and institutional salespeople left at the newly named Prudential Equity Group weren't quite sure the deal was as good as Strangfeld portrayed. Liz Dunn, a star apparel analyst, noted:

> The sale of the retail brokerage to Wachovia led a lot of the troops to say, "How are we making money anymore?" There was communication from the top down about the rationale, but it seemed to me that that was

a big piece of how we made money, and so I was struggling to figure out how we would make money going forward and why they didn't want the institutional piece as well. It surprised a lot of us that you would separate the two.

Even though the retail brokerage unit had lost money recently, the commissions the unit generated helped pay for the entire group. Results from the deal for the first full year after the merger were not encouraging. While Prudential's 38 percent share had generated $172 million in pretax income in 2004, charges related to the merger actually left the division with a $245 million loss (see Exhibit 1.3).[19] To make matters worse, Prudential also had to deal with accusations of illegal market timing trading.

It was in November of 2003 that the Securities and Exchange Commission (SEC) filed charges against Prudential's retail brokerage for engaging in market timing trades with mutual funds.[20] The SEC alleged that Prudential's brokers had engaged in frequent buying and selling of mutual fund shares to exploit short-term swings in the market and differences in closing times in international markets. The trading practices went explicitly against many funds' prospectuses, which specified that their goal was to maximize returns over the long term. While Prudential hadn't settled with the SEC on the charges, it set aside an accrual in the summer of 2005 for a potential fine. This accrual, combined with continuing transition costs due to the merger with Wachovia, contributed to a $255 million loss in 2005.

However, by early 2006 the joint venture appeared to be turning the corner. The merger was nearly complete, and transition costs for the first quarter would be minimal. Industry observers expected that the deal would finally begin bringing in a consistent positive cash flow to the Equity Group.

Exhibit 1.3 Results from Wachovia Joint Venture in millions of dollars.*

	Q1 2004	Q2 2004	Q3 2004	Q4 2004	Q1 2005	Q2 2005	Q3 2005	Q4 2005
Pretax income from 38% share	$54	36	28	54	15	47	59	61
Net profit (loss) after charges	$(14)	(80)	(76)	(75)	15	(97)	31	(204)

* Voxant Fair Disclosure Wire, Final Prudential Earnings Conference Calls 2004–2005, via Factiva, accessed February 8, 2008.

SOURCE: Sam, Ali, "Ex-Pru Staffer Charged by SEC," Star Ledger, November 5, 2003, via Factiva, retrieved on August 3, 2007.

The Demise of Equity Research

Even with some profit coming from the Wachovia joint venture, head of research Steve Buell knew that Prudential would have to find an alternative funding source for research or make a substantial investment into the firm's trading capabilities, in all likelihood requiring an investment from Prudential's corporate headquarters.

In June of 2006, Buell announced that he would be leaving the firm after five years as head of research. Prudential Equities head Michael Shea appointed Stephanie Link, then senior vice president of institutional sales, to be the new director of research. Over the following months, Link and Shea weren't able to strengthen the position of research at Prudential. Bonuses at Prudential for 2006 had been down by as much as 30 percent, even as the market appreciated. Analysts began to leave. In March of 2007, star analyst Michael Mayo left with five of his team members to join Deutsche Bank.

In April, Prudential started shopping the research department around. Potential buyers included Royal Bank of Scotland, Santander, and BNP Paribas. Senior management contemplated a management buyout of the research department. Once private, the new firm could sell its research directly to buy-side firms without having to worry about trading commissions and even pursue resources set aside for independent research from the Global Settlement for at least four years, which might be long enough to stabilize the business model and establish a strong client base. However, there was no guarantee that Prudential's best analysts and sales people would stay after a buyout, and an incentive for the best to move to a new company would be very expensive.

Unable to finalize a deal, Prudential decided to close its research department along with sales and trading on June 6, despite the fact that Prudential's research department had been ranked twelfth or better for the last seven years. Over 400 employees were laid off, including thirty-three senior analysts, at a cost of $110 million in severance packages. Rich Linville, a former Prudential salesman, remarked:

> The writing was on the wall. Prudential had a trading platform for a business model that no longer existed. We were like a 400-pound person who lost 200 pounds but was still trying to wear the same clothes.

Conclusions

The Prudential story illustrates many of the important changes that have taken place in the relations among brokerage, investment banking, and sell-side equity research during the last twenty-five years. CEO Bob Beck's vision that Prudential could be a "one-stop shop" for customer's financial and insurance needs predated the emergence of global financial powerhouses such as Citigroup and JPMorgan Chase. Its demise raises questions about the viability of the strategy and the challenges in execution. The firm's foray into investment banking was a direct response to competitors recognizing the financial benefits from leveraging banking and equity research. Prudential's subsequent exit from investment banking successfully anticipated a downturn in the sector and concerns about conflicts of interest between investment banking and equity research. Finally, its decision to abandon equity research altogether came at a time when others in the industry were raising questions about the viability of sell-side research. We examine many of the questions about sell-side research raised by the Prudential story.

2

What Do Analysts Do, and How Are They Managed?

In *Exile on Wall Street*, top-ranked banking and finance analyst Michael Mayo—who for a time worked at Prudential Securities—described his job succinctly:

> [The analyst's] job is to study publicly traded financial firms and decide which ones would make the best investments. My research goes out to institutional investors: mutual fund companies, university endowments, public-employee retirement funds, hedge funds, private pensions, and other organizations with large amounts of money. Some individuals I meet with manage $10 billion or more, which they invest in banks and other stocks. If they believe what I say, they invest accordingly, trading through my firm.[1]

Mayo developed a reputation for his willingness to express controversial points of view, even if it ruffled the feathers of executives at the large banks he covered. For example, he was disparaged for calling the bottom in bank stocks in 1994, although he was subsequently proved correct. He put a sell on bank stocks in 1999, and he criticized executives at the largest U.S. banks for their lavish pay and mismanagement well before the subprime mortgage crisis.

As we saw for Prudential, sell-side analysts provide services to both buy-side investors (including managers of pension funds, mutual funds, and hedge funds) and managers of the stocks they cover. To buy-side clients they provide research ideas. To company managers they help make a liquid and orderly market for their stocks, facilitating the raising of new capital and the trading of outstanding shares. In this chapter, we examine in more detail the job of sell-side equity research analysts and how they are managed.

In performing their research function, analysts typically specialize in covering companies in a particular industry. Their insights come from analyzing industry data and company filings and from interacting with executives of the companies they cover, clients, their own sales force members and traders, and other analysts. Sell-side research department managers look to hire people who will become leading analysts. In making hiring decisions, research managers look for intellect, work ethic, entrepreneurship, risk taking, and communication skills. Other areas of expertise, such as industry experience, are also taken into consideration. Hiring strategies vary across firms, with some hiring established star analysts from other firms and others hiring rookies who are then developed into stars. Research managers also provide analysts with training and mentoring to help them build their franchise, particularly for firms that develop talent internally rather than hiring stars. Finally, strong research departments spend considerable time and resources evaluating analyst performance and determining analyst compensation.

The Work of an Analyst

In a 1999 interview with *The Wall Street Journal*, Lehman Brothers' analyst Nicholas Lobaccaro described a typical day for a sell-side analyst. Although much has changed in the industry since 1999, analysts continue to perform the same fundamental daily activities described in this study. Lobaccaro's narration enumerates the important dimensions to analysts' work, including producing the research product itself, servicing clients, and marketing their coverage companies.[2]

For analysts, a typical day in the office begins with a review of the morning news to determine whether there is anything new that could affect the stocks they cover. Most brokerage firms and investment banks hold a morning meeting, often at 7:30 a.m., at which analysts communicate their ideas to the firm's sales force and summarize recently published written reports. The sales force then passes this information on to the firm's institutional clients before the market opens at 9:30 a.m. Former telecom industry analyst Dan Reingold described the early morning activity at Merrill Lynch:

> As 9:30 approached, the trading desks always became frantic, with traders yelling orders and market rumors being tossed back and forth across Merrill's football field of a trading floor. For me, in the quiet of my office 16 floors higher, it was also a tense time of the day. Had any telecom companies issued press releases? Were any of my stocks making unexpected moves? Had I missed any news? Was anyone else announcing an opinion change? Ideally, I wouldn't find myself on the wrong end of the information flow, but it did happen.[3]

Following the market opening, analysts might spend time in the office with colleagues discussing ongoing work, reviewing drafts of reports, and planning next steps. Analysts use this office time to read, write reports, and work on financial models. They may also hold conference calls with buy-side clients and with management from companies under coverage, field incoming calls and e-mails from clients, and meet with visiting clients who want to discuss a particular company or research report. Analysts' schedules may be interrupted by unforeseen events that affect the stocks of the companies they cover—unexpected macroeconomic data or a rumor about lackluster sales—and require issuing a written report or passing their commentaries on to the sales force.

However, analysts spend 30 percent or more of their time out of the office traveling, visiting clients or companies under coverage, and attending conferences. On the road, analysts usually schedule back-to-back meetings with clients in the same city or with executives at the same company. They also remain in close contact with the office to ensure that their research colleagues and sales reps are aware of any new information and to learn of new market developments.

Analyst Research

Sell-side research analysts have been described as Wall Street's "financial detectives."[4] They study public companies with a view to advising their clients on which stocks to buy and sell. Michael Nathanson, a media analyst at Sanford C. Bernstein, described the analyst position as similar to that of a reporter. He stated, "You might go out and spend four months talking to people who are in the industry, getting a sense of what they're seeing and what's going on."[5] Analysts study macroeconomic trends and industry dynamics, evaluate the financial and strategic decisions of company management, and review financial statements to understand company performance. They speak regularly to company management; visit manufacturing plants, distribution facilities, and retail outlets; and interview suppliers, distributors, and customers.

A typical analyst follows ten to twenty companies in a single industry, although the number of companies covered varies widely by sector, by research firm, and over time. Analysts are generally hired to cover an industry group, often one on which they have significant knowledge from prior work or educational experience. Analysts who are hired without knowledge of a particular industry will generally be assigned one based on the firm's personnel needs. Once they begin to cover an industry, analysts rarely move from one industry group to another.

Analysts communicate their research to clients in the form of written reports that include qualitative assessments of industry dynamics and the firm's business model; quantitative forecasts of earnings, financial models, and target stock prices; and an investment recommendation. Forecasts of quarterly earnings and revenues are typically issued for as many as eight quarters ahead, whereas target price forecast horizons are usually for the following twelve months. Analysts write a new research piece every few days, each of which can range from a one- to five-page news-related publication, generally referred to as a "note," to a fifty-page in-depth company report. Each research firm has its own standard template, but the front page usually includes the brokerage and analyzed firms' names, the analyst's name, the report name, summary market data, summary financial data, earnings estimates, an investment recommendation, and a summary of the report's findings.

One- to five-page notes are the most common written output. Analysts produce them quickly (often in a matter of hours) in response to a piece of news, such as a quarterly earnings release, an acquisition, or a change in key personnel. The purpose of a note is to summarize the event, describe any anticipated change in company fundamentals as a result of the event, and reaffirm (or if necessary, change) an analyst's investment recommendation on the company. Analysts also write upgrade or downgrade notes to announce a change in their investment recommendations on particular stocks or sectors and to detail the rationale for the changes.

Longer reports represent months of research and analysis; they present a thorough overview of a company, industry, product line, or strategy.

When analysts initiate coverage of a company or sector, they normally "launch" coverage with an in-depth report that details their investment thesis. Analysts also periodically write "white papers," thorough analyses of a particular issue or topic. Some firms, such as Bernstein, are particularly well known for their in-depth reports. Sallie Krawcheck, former director of research at Bernstein, noted that the "Bernstein Black Book" is known for its dense analysis:

> Everybody knows this is how the Bernstein Black Book looks. Not like other firms' reports, where the retail reports have pictures of stores on them, and the leisure stuff has the guy gambling. Everybody knows this is the Bernstein report.[6]

Once written, research reports and notes are sent by the analysts to buy-side clients via e-mail, fax, or mail. Analyst reports are also forwarded electronically to database services (such as Thomson Reuters's FirstCall), which aggregate sell-side research reports. Buy-side investors are then able to have access to reports directly via these online databases.

At the heart of analyst reports is the investment recommendation. Each investment firm has its own standard language for recommendations. For example, for many years Merrill Lynch employed an alphanumeric coding system designed to communicate their analysts' zero- to twelve-month recommendation on stocks, their estimated price volatility, and their dividend outlook.[7] However, recommendations at all firms can be broadly classified into "buy," "hold," and "sell" categories.

Most firms have a formal review process that their analysts are required to complete before changing recommendations on a stock. One Lehman analyst described his firm's process as follows: "If I decided to change a recommendation, I had to present my thesis to the investment committee and answer a barrage of questions to explain why I was changing. Incomplete or unsatisfactory reports were sent back to the drawing board."[8]

The recommendations and forecasts included in analysts' reports reflect analysts' understanding of the firm's industry, business model, strategy, and management quality. A 2011 study by Groysberg, Healy, Nohria, and Serafeim examines the qualitative factors that underlie analysts' forecasts. Based on a survey of 967 analysts covering 837 companies, they conclude that key qualitative drivers of analysts' forecasts and recommendations include their assessments of industry performance (notably industry growth and competitiveness) and the firm's own capabilities, including its ability to execute strategy, the quality of its top management, its innovation, and its culture, particularly whether it is performance driven.[9]

Interestingly, when surveyed, buy-side investors repeatedly indicate that they rely less on the investment recommendations and forecasts, per se, of sell-side analysts and more on their ideas and industry knowledge. Joe Amato, former director of research at Lehman Brothers, concluded, "Our clients don't ask us to pick stocks for them; they do that. They come to us for nuances, insight, shades of gray, and for things that analysts know because they have original insight into their field."[10] Another sell-side department head opined:

Today, I think the role of the analyst is very focused on a couple of things. One is industry expertise. If you have a generalist portfolio manager or even a buy-side analyst who's covering a fairly broad amount of stocks, when they run a screen or get interested in a stock they may not be really familiar with the sub-industry or the details of the company, the business model . . . The sell-side analyst, on average covers about seven stocks per professional, 15 stocks per team. They are much deeper on any name than anyone on the buy-side and definitely any portfolio manager. And you may not love their research or their stock picking, but they tend to have a lot of industry expertise . . . [knowledge of] industry structure, who the players are, what are the business models, what are the strengths and weaknesses of each model.

Michael Herzig, former head of equity research at Merrill Lynch, asserted, "Research that sells is research that can make people think. And what makes a portfolio manager or buy-side analyst think are things that they hadn't really considered before—ideas or approaches that call into question their existing beliefs."[11]

A 2012 study by Maber, Groysberg, and Healy provides further insight into what sell-side analysts do and how they spend their time. The study uses data for a midsized investment bank from 2004 to 2007 and examines which analyst activities generate incremental trading commissions for their firms. The median analyst in the study covered sixteen companies that together generated $180,000 in monthly trading commissions for the analyst's firm. In a given month, the representative analyst issued one major new report, and twelve company-specific notes that included five new/updated EPS forecasts (one of which deviated dramatically from the consensus) and one recommendation change. Maber, Groysberg, and

Healy find that increases in the number of written notes, divergent forecasts, and changes in recommendations that analysts issued were related to increases in trading commissions for the stocks they covered, thereby benefiting their employers.[12]

Client Services

Sell-side analysts also provide a variety of customized services to the buy-side investment community and to corporate clients. These include private communications with leading clients, customized research products, participation in investment banking transactions (at least prior to the Global Settlement, in 2003), and arranging opportunities for buy-side clients to meet with corporate managers of the firms they cover.

Private Conversations.   Sell-side analysts communicate regularly with their leading clients through phone conversations, e-mails, and personal visits. One-on-one conversations with buy-side clients allow analysts to field questions about their research and ideas, which is valuable to the client, but it also allows the analysts to test and subsequently refine their ideas.

Most firms require analysts to plan and log their client contacts. For example, Lehman Brothers required analysts to record the number of client visits, calls, and e-mails, the names of clients contacted, and the key topics discussed. (See Exhibits 2.1 and 2.2 for summary client marketing data for Lehman Brothers.) They then stored this data centrally and made it available to other analysts, sales force members, and traders. Maber, Groysberg, and Healy (2012) report that, in a given month, the median analyst at their midsized sample firm made 120 calls to buy-side clients.[13]

Customized Research.   In addition to their regular research reports, analysts and brokerage firms produce research that is customized to client needs. For example, Leerink Swann, a health care specialist research and brokerage firm established in the mid-1990s, was founded on the premise that sell-side health care research was failing to meet the needs of buy-side managers. Rather than relying solely on mass-produced research reports, Leerink Swann's founders established MEDACorp, a captive network of 30,000 vetted doctors, who met with investors and responded to specific client questions on emerging technologies, new products, and other areas of interest. By 1999, *Institutional Investor* ranked Leerink Swann #1

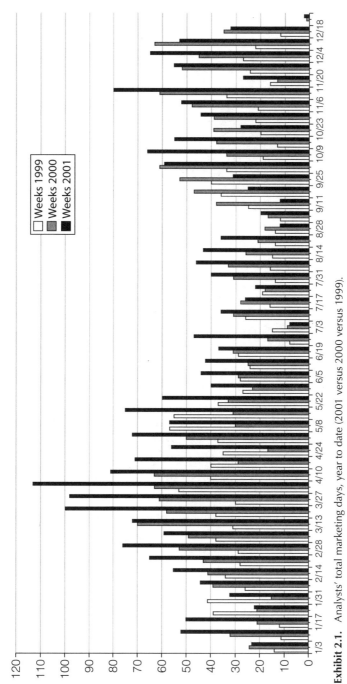

Exhibit 2.1. Analysts' total marketing days, year to date (2001 versus 2000 versus 1999).

SOURCE: Boris Groysberg and Ashish Nanda, "Lehman Brothers (D): Reemergence of the Equity Research Department," HBS No. 406-090 (Boston: Harvard Business School Publishing, 2006), p. 23.

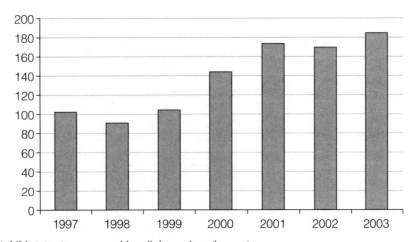

Exhibit 2.2. Average monthly calls by analysts (by year).

SOURCE: Boris Groysberg and Ashish Nanda, "Lehman Brothers (D): Reemergence of the Equity Research Department," HBS No. 406-090 (Boston: Harvard Business School Publishing, 2006), p. 24.

in regional health care. (See Chapter 3 for a more detailed discussion of *Institutional Investor* rankings.)

Participating in Investment Banking Transactions.   Beginning in the 1980s, investment bankers started to utilize analysts' expertise in considering how to position an IPO (initial public offering) or an M&A (merger and acquisition) transaction. By the mid-1990s, analysts were devoting more of their time to investment banking activities, particularly in the so-called new economy sectors such as Internet and telecom. As M&A and equity issuance volumes increased dramatically with the technology boom, so too did investment banking revenues. Skyrocketing investment banking profits gave investment bankers greater power within their firms and provided increased funding for research.

At the height of the tech stock boom, sell-side analysts were expected to help pitch new investment banking accounts for their firms. The analyst's credibility with investors and ability to help market the transaction to investors were considered a key part of the sales pitch. Once awarded an investment banking contract, the analyst would assist the company in preparing IPO documentation and marketing presentations and would travel with the company around the globe on "road shows" at which management marketed their equity offering to investors. Former analyst Dan Reingold described this phenomenon:

As the 1990s went on, the planets of the bankers and the analysts slowly began to orbit more closely around each other. While there had always been interactions, now the bankers, long the alpha dogs, were beginning to realize that research could wag its tail too. If used in the right way, those nerds in the back room might help make them big money.[14]

A number of star analysts, such as Mary Meeker and Jack Grubman (defined as "stars" due to their high ranking by *Institutional Investor*), became driving forces behind their firms' investment banking activities during this period. A 2001 article in *Fortune* detailed Mary Meeker's role at Morgan Stanley:

> Because the Internet was so new, investors wanted a credible source to explain it to them—and tell them which companies to invest in. And who was more credible than Meeker? She became the gold standard, the person who gave a company instant stature merely by her association with it. Thus, even as she was chasing companies for Morgan Stanley, companies were chasing her. "The bankers were superfluous," says Todd Wagner, former CEO of Broadcast.com, recalling his company's decision to go with Morgan when it went public in 1998. "Our rationale was, if we went with Morgan Stanley, we'd get Mary Meeker and we'd get a lot of attention."[15]

A rival banker added, "We were not competing with Morgan at all. We were competing with Mary Meeker. The clients made that very clear."[16]

Since the Global Settlement was enacted in 2003, such collaboration has been greatly curtailed and now occurs only within the parameters of the so-called Chinese walls that, as required by the new regulations, separate investment banking and research departments.[17] However, many firms still require that their analyst in the relevant industry vet a proposed equity offering before the firm will commit to underwrite the offering.

Organizing Private Meetings between Buy-Side and Corporate Clients.   Finally, sell-side research analysts use their firms' convening power to create opportunities for their most profitable buy-side clients to meet with company managers in small group settings. This is accomplished by hosting investor conferences to which firms invite both buy-side clients and company managers, by setting up "field trips" during which investors can visit company retail outlets or manufacturing plants, and by sponsoring non-deal road shows, whereby analysts arrange for company managers to visit buy-side investors and update them or introduce them to their company. In this way, sell-side analysts act as intermediaries, providing a valuable service to both their buy-side and corporate clients. One buy-side analyst described the benefit of these types of services:

> I just went out to California. A sell-side analyst hosted a trip to visit a company that I cover. I could have set that trip up myself, but because it was already set up and there were eight other buy-side analysts going, it was just as easy to go on that trip. I had a lot of questions of my own, but the sell-side analyst also asked a lot of great questions of her own which I found helpful. I go on trips like that a lot. It's a great way to meet other buy-side analysts and get their views on the industry and what names they like and don't like and why.

In the post–Regulation Fair Disclosure era (discussed in Chapter 5), organizing such trips has become an increasingly important part of analysts' client service responsibilities, prompting critics to dismiss modern analysts as "cruise directors."[18]

Consistent with buy-side clients citing "corporate access" as a key value-add that the sell-side provides, Maber, Groysberg, and Healy (2012) find that increases in these types of activities by analysts were positively related to client votes used to determine next quarter's commissions.

Leveraging Support Services within the Firm

Successful analysts leverage the resources provided by their own firms to undertake research and to market their findings. Analysts typically receive support in their research tasks from research associates and/or junior analysts. Junior analysts and associates perform similar tasks, and the titles are often used interchangeably. However, some research associates are hired directly from undergraduate programs, while junior analysts tend to have prior work experience and MBAs.

Research associates and junior analysts are generally hired by research department management and are then matched with an analyst based on skill set and personality fit. As Sanford C. Bernstein's manager of research support Sara Mahoney described, "Sometimes an analyst will want someone with strong accounting skills, or strong writing skills, depending on what the analyst himself is weak in."[19] The ratio of research associates/

junior analysts to analysts varies by firm and sector but often falls in the range of 1:1 to 3:1.

Research associates and junior analysts help senior analysts stay on top of company news, field client calls, write reports, communicate with the sales force and traders, and update financial models. (See Exhibit 2.3 for a typical day for a research associate.) The way in which work is divided between an analyst and the analyst's support staff is almost wholly at the discretion of the analyst. Some junior analysts are given one to three companies to cover on their own, with only minimal supervision, while at the other end of the spectrum they are relegated to inputting data into spreadsheets.

Analysts and their "juniors" function as a team, with the analyst's name at the top of all work products. Analysts are responsible for the career development of their staff, for detailing the job description, and for providing the bulk of the input on their performance reviews. Given this close working relationship, it is common for senior analysts who move from one firm to another to take their junior analysts and research associates with them.

Compensation for junior analysts and research associates varies, but in recent years associates have earned about $100,000 while junior analysts have earned from $100,000 to $350,000. Senior analysts are responsible for determining annual bonuses for juniors and associates (within a range

Exhibit 2.3　Morgan Stanley Dean Witter, on the typical job day.

Associate, Equity Research, Morgan Stanley	
8:30 am	Arrive at work; review any news concerning the 21 aerospace companies that Morgan Stanley researches. Talk to traders on the floor; brief sales staff on any changes to particular companies.
9:30 am	Stock market opens.
10:00 am	Begin meetings with institutional investors on the benefits and perils of investing in various aerospace industries; prepare reports on company developments.
12:00 pm	Lunch at desk.
12:30 pm	Conduct financial models on various companies to forecast their earnings. Conduct company research, which "involves reading industry journals, interviewing industry experts, and even occasionally traveling to visit company facilities."
3:00 pm	Continue meetings and telephone calls with institutional investors.
5:45 pm	Discuss investment and sales strategies with various Morgan Stanley investment bankers.
6:00 pm	Work with boss, a senior analyst, to review financial predictions.
7:00 pm	Edit company reports for publication on a financial wire service—one hour per company.
10:30 pm	Go home.

SOURCE: Morgan Stanley Dean Witter, Vault Reports, Inc., 80 Fifth Avenue, 11th Floor, New York, NY 10011, (212) 366-4212, www.vaultreports.com.

set by department management). As one former research associate described, "In terms of compensation, it was really based almost entirely on what your analyst thought of you. If he thought you were doing a good job, that's what they relied on to come up with what your annual bonus would be."

Analysts also receive support from institutional salespeople and traders at their own firms. Prior to the 1950s, there were no institutional sales forces, and "selling analysts" were solely responsible for communicating their research message to clients. Today, however, institutional salespeople are responsible for summarizing analyst research and for relaying key points to buy-side clients. Salespeople also arrange visits and conference calls with clients and keep analysts updated on client thinking—which stocks they are watching and want to be updated on. Without an effective sales force, an analyst would need to devote even more time to client marketing. As former analyst Steve Galbraith commented, "Salespeople's influence is huge on whether or not a research analyst's message gets out. A great sales force is one of the big competitive advantages any firm can have."[20] Consistent with this, Maber, Groysberg, and Healy (2012) find that, in a given month, a typical analyst at a midsized firm made six presentations to the brokerage firm's sales force and that these presentations were positively associated with the generation of commission revenues for the analysts' portfolio of stocks.

Traders inform analysts about news from the trading floor, including large trades, key short-term trends, and individual clients' buying and selling activities. Jeff Leerink, CEO of Leerink Swann, commented, "If you're trading stocks, you're in the flow . . . There's always valuable information coming off the trading floor."[21]

Communication among analysts, traders, and salespeople within a firm is an almost continuous process. It starts with the previously mentioned morning meeting; then, throughout the day, analysts update salespeople and traders on major news events using the internal intercom system referred to as a "squawk box'" or via blast e-mails.

Managing Research Departments

To build and sustain a successful research department, firms have to hire the right people, provide them with suitable training and mentoring, and develop effective ways to evaluate and reward them.

Analyst Hiring

Prior to the 1950s, newly hired analysts were often new or recent college graduates, with virtually no Wall Street experience, who used the position as a training ground for careers in finance. Beginning in the late 1950s, research firms began hiring more experienced analysts, often with a background in the industry that they were to cover. Today's research analysts possess diverse academic and employment backgrounds. Many have advanced degrees, primarily MBAs but also MDs, JDs, and PhDs. Many are hired from the industries they will cover—with research management often valuing industry knowledge over finance experience. For example, Sanford C. Bernstein media analyst Michael Nathanson came from Time Warner and chemicals analyst Nick Henderson from British Petroleum.

Some firms focus on developing junior talent with a view to promoting junior analysts as opportunities arise. Others prefer to hire experienced analysts from small regional firms or highly rated "star" analysts from leading Wall Street banks. Many firms use a combination of these hiring strategies.

Firms with a strong unique corporate culture, regarded as a key competitive advantage, frequently adopt the "homegrown" approach: They hire individuals without experience, train them to be analysts, and subsequently promote the most talented. Such is the case at Sanford C. Bernstein. Founder Sanford Bernstein commented, "We tried in the beginning to get experienced and finished analysts . . . but we weren't satisfied and so we backed into having to train our own."[22] Post-2003, Credit Suisse has put increased emphasis on promoting research analysts from within after having a strategy of hiring stars from its competitors, and by 2009 25 percent of the firm's ranked analysts had started at Credit Suisse as associates.[23]

Sara Karlen, former head of human resources for research at Merrill Lynch, described her firm's strategy in 2005 of using internal promotions rather than external hires:

> The senior analysts are important, but there is just as much value placed on the junior analyst and the talent pipeline. There is a great deal of emphasis on organic growth. Gone are the days when every time we had an opening, there was a rush to the outside to fill it. We have very talented people that we want to provide opportunities to, and we want people in research to see this as a long-term career and not just a five-year relationship.[24]

A former research associate at Thomas Weisel Partners, which adopted a similar strategy, pointed out that one benefit of focusing on internal promotions is to motivate junior staff members:

> Something like two out of every five associates have been promoted to an analyst. It was used as motivation because Weisel wanted to promote from within, and that would essentially be what they would tell you, "Work hard and we'll make you an analyst if you really prove yourself."

However, for firms in a hurry to fill analyst positions or to boost the research department's performance statistics, the homegrown approach is often considered too slow. In these instances, hiring star analysts from competitors is the preferred strategy for many firms. Such was the case at Lehman Brothers in 1999 as Joe Amato, global head of research, and Steve Hash, head of U.S. equities research, looked to upgrade the talent in the research department and set higher expectations. As Hash recalled,

> From early 1999 to mid-2000, we hired eight ranked analysts . . . That is about the upper limit on how many ranked-analyst hires you can make in a short period of time. If one analyzes the pattern of hiring senior II-ranked analysts, one rarely sees more than five hires in a year. The process is just too hard.[25]

Combining this selective hiring strategy with massive internal development efforts allowed the firm to move from number eight in the *Institutional Investor* poll to a top-five ranking. By 2003, it was number one.

A recent study by Groysberg, Lee, and Nanda questions the value of hiring star analysts from competitor firms. On average, star analysts who switched banks underperformed star analysts who stayed put for at least five years. This study shows that star analysts who moved from one brokerage firm to another with comparable resources and prestige experienced a post-move decline in performance that typically lasted two years. The study finds, however, that this performance decline did not occur when the star analysts brought their colleague(s) with them when moving. In contrast, analysts who moved on their own typically saw their performance decline for as many as five years. The post-move decline in performance was also exacerbated when analysts moved to a firm with lesser resources and prestige. In such instances, the decline also persisted for five years. In contrast, star analysts who moved to firms with better capabilities saw no notable performance decline.[26]

The process of hiring analysts tends to be lengthy and involved. Firms generally engage headhunters to find interested candidates and to manage the hiring process. They then bring in qualified candidates for numerous rounds of interviews with research department management, other analysts, and, often, traders and salespeople. At Sanford C. Bernstein, for example, the hiring process regularly takes a full year; candidates on headhunters' lists often come in for as many as twenty interviews.

As discussed, qualities that managers look for in hiring analysts include intellect, work ethic, entrepreneurship, a willingness to take risks, and communication skills. Fred Fraenkel, a former manager of Lehman Brothers' research department, explained the "four qualities" test he used when interviewing analyst candidates:

> I tried to figure out whether the interviewee had the intellectual capacity and the work ethic to become an industry expert. If those two qualities didn't exist, then nothing else mattered. The third question was whether the interviewee was capable of representing those two qualities to clients, orally or in writing, so that they could be recognized. All you can do in this business is call, visit, or write—that's it; there's no other way to gain recognition for expertise. The fourth part was our magic bullet. I asked myself whether the interviewee was someone people were going to like. And if he or she wasn't, I would take a pass.[27]

The unstructured nature of the analyst position means that analysts have to be self-motivated. They need to have drive and to set their own objectives and time horizons. Research department managers can help in setting long-range objectives or putting in place performance tracking systems, but on a daily basis no one stands over an analyst's shoulder. Analysts need to establish their own priorities, manage their own schedules, and set their own deadlines.

A key priority for an analyst is to build a franchise. To do so, the analyst has to be an entrepreneur. The analyst's firm brand can provide a foot in the door with respect to client access, but ultimately the analyst needs to build his or her own credibility to be successful. As an entrepreneur, the analyst has to understand the market, build a research product that investors want to read, market the product to clients through calls and visits, and build name recognition through media exposure and ranking in industry polls. Former Lehman analyst Kim Wallace opined:

> What [did] it take at Lehman Brothers to succeed and be a star analyst? The easy part of it [was] you had to own your franchise. You [had] to be

an entrepreneur in knowing what's important to the client base, trends in your sector that might lead to change . . . anticipating those changes, and then communicating them thoroughly, repetitiously, until people [got] the message. Sometimes, there's so much information that flows at buy-side analysts from all corners that it is difficult to differentiate yourself. One way that you do it is by repeating what you believe to be good calls. And, of course, you develop relations with people who listened to you the first time around, so that stuff was a given.

Finally, analysts need to be willing to take risks, to make recommendations that sometimes go against the market's current perception, with the knowledge that they may be wrong and that clients and managers may be unhappy with them. As Michael Nathanson asserted:

> They want people who are OK when they're wrong. In this job, you're going to be wrong—hopefully less than half the time; that's your benchmark. It's almost like blackjack: if you can beat the house half the time, you're OK. But you're going to lose at times. You're going to get something wrong. And you have to be able to deal with that, and to go back again and talk to your clients, and say, "Look, I got that wrong. Here's what I missed," and be able to be honest about yourself.[28]

Training Analysts

Most brokerage houses offer some type of training for new analysts, varying widely in length and level of formality. At one end of the spectrum, Sanford C. Bernstein gives its new analysts approximately one year to learn their industry and the analyst job. This training is informal and individually driven. The new hires are expected to study their coverage companies, read the research of other Bernstein analysts, and seek out advice from their colleagues. Bernstein analyst Vladimir Zlotnikov explained, "You take somebody who is smart, who has proven to be successful in other areas, who is motivated enough to work hard, you leave them alone, you help them slightly with the process, but you really allow them to develop their own independent point of view, their voice."[29] Sallie Krawcheck, director of research at Bernstein in the 1990s, added, "We bring them in and pay them hundreds of thousands of dollars to sit in their office and learn!"[30]

Other firms offer more formalized training. Analysts and junior analysts who are hired directly from business school participate in firmwide training designed specifically for new MBAs. This training, which is full

Exhibit 2.4   Gary Black's eight simple rules to success as an analyst: Sanford C. Bernstein new analyst guide.

1. Be first.
2. Be proactive.
3. Be value-added.
4. Be visible.
5. Be decisive.
6. Be opportunistic.
7. Be clear.
8. Be humble.
Objective: Dominate your category

SOURCE: Boris Groysberg, Anahita Hashemi, "Sanford C. Bernstein: Growing Pains," HBS No. 405-011 (Boston: Harvard Business School Publishing, 2004), p. 28.

time and lasts several weeks, includes an introduction to the firm, compliance, accounting and financial analysis, and presentation skills. Many research departments also provide their own training for new hires. As one analyst recalled, "It was a week of training covering communications skills, accounting, valuation models, standard investment banking research training." Some firms provide further training to assist new analysts in preparing for regulatory exams. Analysts are generally required to pass the Series 7, 63, 86, and 87 exams prior to communicating with clients.

For experienced analysts, most firms offer ongoing training. Some conduct training programs to help analysts move up the *Institutional Investor* rankings. For example, at Bernstein, Gary Black, a tobacco analyst, shared his "Eight Simple Rules to Success as an Analyst" with less experienced analysts (see Exhibit 2.4). At one point, Lehman Brothers offered an "Accelerated Marketing Class" to selected analysts. Steve Hash described the program:

> What I had learned . . . was that we should run "accelerated marketing training" just as if it were an accredited college course. We would have a clear start, a clear end, and seven modules in between. It would be an intensive, seven weeks, two-hours-per-week program. We would have a class of ten to fifteen analysts—no larger, no smaller. Too small, it's not as effective; too large, it becomes out of control. The program would use handouts to focus on marketing—it would be about working with the sales force and making an impression on the buy side.[31]

Evaluating Analysts

In many respects, analyst performance is assessed continuously and in a highly public way. Dan Reingold, a former telecom analyst, explained:

Unlike many people in the corporate world, investors and their advisors got graded every day. If I missed some news or made a bad call, I'd hear about it immediately, first from the trading prices of the stocks and then from an unhappy money manager who'd followed my advice or a . . . salesman who'd pitched it hard.[32]

However, most organizations also have formal annual review processes in place that assess analyst performance using a wide range of metrics. In conducting these assessments, research managers use quantitative and qualitative data points from internal and external sources. (See Exhibits 2.5, 2.6, and 2.7 for a sample analyst performance review form used by two investment banks.) Based on analysis of these data points, research management assigns analysts an overall performance rank that is then used to determine annual bonuses. While some firms provide to their analysts the exact methodology used in determining how the bonus pool is divided among analysts, most do not disclose detailed compensation calculations, particularly if there is subjectivity in the evaluations.

Among the data used to evaluate analysts are internal performance ratings completed annually by analysts' peers, supervisors, and support staff. These evaluations measure everything from industry and company knowledge to contribution on collaborative projects, willingness to mentor juniors, and commitment to ethical standards. Research departments also track a wide number of data items for analysts, such as the number of client calls, the number of pages written, the performance of investment recommendations, and trade volume in the analyst's recommended stocks. Analysts are often asked to put together an annual business plan with their key objectives for the next twelve months. Plan objectives may include increasing the number of companies under coverage or writing a minimum number of reports and are used as a benchmark for evaluating subsequent performance.

Industry polls represent a key external or market evaluation of analyst performance. Most notable among these is the annual poll of buy-side analysts and portfolio managers conducted by *Institutional Investor*. The importance of this poll in the analyst assessment process cannot be stressed enough. One Lehman analyst referred to his firm's assessment process as "*II* or die."[33] Greenwich Associates and Reuters also publish industry rankings based on a poll of institutional investors. *The Wall Street Journal* initiated an annual sell-side analyst ranking in 1993. This ranking is based on accuracy of earnings estimates and performance of stock picks.

Buy-side investors also contribute to the assessment process via broker votes. The results of these voting processes are generally communicated

Market Share in Trading Commissions (Percentage)

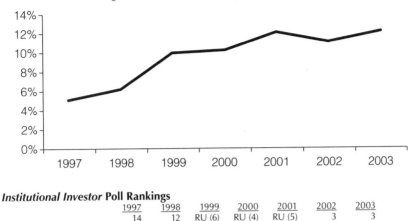

Institutional Investor Poll Rankings

	1997	1998	1999	2000	2001	2002	2003
	14	12	RU (6)	RU (4)	RU (5)	3	3

Research Votes from clients
(represents quartile within Rubin, Stern, and Hertz Research Dept.)

1997	3rd Quartile
1998	3rd Quartile
1999	1st Quartile
2000	1st Quartile
2001	1st Quartile
2002	1st Quartile
2003	1st Quartile

Common comments from clients

- We like him for his industry knowledge rather than stock picking skills
- Written research is organized, clear, concise
- Effective in client meetings—makes strong case for the thesis/stocks
- Need more help with stock selection
- Solid work. Keep up the great work!
- Very proactive and has value added comments
- Good quarterly work
- Great company meetings
- Would like to hear from him more
- Good resource for industry information
- He makes bold anti-consensus calls
- I respect Peter for not wavering
- He is good for long-term investors
- He correctly identifies winners but not losers
- He has become a high-profile analyst because of his calls but lately it is hard to get in touch with him
- He walked away from Intel too early
- He is good at identifying market shifts and how the stocks will trade at inflection points

Survey of Institutional Salesmen & Traders
(# represents quartile within Rubin, Stern, and Hertz Research Dept.)

	1997	1998	1999	2000	2001	2002	2003
Sector Expertise	4	3	2	1	1	1	1
Stock Picking	4	3	3	3	4	3	3
Marketing	3	2	3	3	2	1	1
Quality of Written Reports	2	2	1	1	1	1	1
Research Ideas	3	3	2	2	1	2	2
Management Access	4	4	4	2	2	1	2
Accessibility/Responsiveness	2	2	1	2	1	1	1
Overall Response	4	3	2	2	1	1	1

Exhibit 2.5. Performance review for Peter Thompson, 2003.

SOURCE: Research director. (Some information has been disguised.)

Exhibit 2.6 Mock analyst profit and loss statement (accounts for 55 percent of the scorecard).

70% of analyst P&L revenues are derived by summing the following on a weighted basis:

	Dollars	Weighting
Client vote revenues[1]	$5,010,633	
Investment manager meeting revenues[2]	$1,002,127	
Client vote + investment manager	$6,012,760	80%
Management access revenues[3]	$10,753,771	20%
Total revenues	$6,960,962	

30% of analyst P&L revenues are based on secondary trading commissions in the analyst's sector:

Trading revenues	$6,052,080
Total revenues	$6,688,298
Direct costs	(734,937)
Revenues: Direct costs	$5,953,361

1. These include revenues generated from the high touch clients and sales-managed clients (including management access and growth opportunities). The clients in this category provide Credit Suisse with detailed feedback, and most provide a breakdown as to how they allocate their total commission dollars among the following services: research services, management access, HOLT, and trade execution. For each analyst, the revenues from an individual client are multiplied by the percentage of value that that client allocates to research and then multiplied by the percentage of total client votes that the individual analyst received. If the client does not provide a breakdown of their perceived value of trade commissions, then the average percentage attributed to research for that client's segment is used as a default in order to calculate analyst revenues. HOLT is a proprietary Credit Suisse database that includes detailed financial information on over 20,000 companies globally. This database is used primarily to perform cash flow–based company valuations. It is included as part of Credit Suisse's overall equities offering; as such, Credit Suisse is expected to be compensated for HOLT via secondary trading commissions.

2. These include the revenues generated by the Institutional Markets segment clients.

3. This category is calculated similarly to client vote revenues. Dollar commissions, per client, are multiplied by the percentage that that client ascribes to management access. That number is then multiplied by the percentage of corporate access events each analyst has doled out.

SOURCE: Boris Groysberg, Paul M. Healy, and Sarah Abbott. "Credit Suisse Group: Managing Equity Research as a Business." Harvard Business School Case 410-073 (Boston: Harvard Business School Publishing, 2005), p. 14.

Exhibit 2.7 Analyst scorecard.

A. Quantifiable metrics

Criteria	Weighting
Analyst P&L	55%
Sales feedback	5%
Trade idea monitor	10%
Performance of recommendations	5%
Cross sector survey	5%
Total quantifiable metrics	**80%**

B. Qualitative metrics

Criteria	Weighting
Product quality, vetting, value added to firmwide initiatives, teamwork, compliance role model, mentoring and development of team, global coordination with research colleagues	20%
Total qualitative metrics	**20%**
Total metrics	**100%**

SOURCE: Boris Groysberg, Paul M. Healy, and Sarah Abbott. "Credit Suisse Group: Managing Equity Research as a Business." Harvard Business School Case 410-073 (Boston: Harvard Business School Publishing, 2005), p. 15.

to sell-side firms in an abbreviated form and used as a factor in the analyst assessment process.

Analyst Compensation

Brokerage firms compensate analysts with a combination of salary, annual bonus, and, in some cases, company stock. The salary component is typically a relatively small piece of the overall compensation package, generally in the $100,000 to $200,000 range. Annual performance bonuses can vary widely by year and by analyst. The aggregate size of the bonus pool for the research department depends primarily on the firm's performance. Research management then divides the pool among analysts based on their rankings awarded from performance reviews. Recently hired analysts, particularly star analysts, may be guaranteed minimum compensation.

A recent study by Groysberg, Healy, and Maber (2011) shows that at a leading investment bank average real sell-side analyst compensation increased dramatically during the late 1990s to a peak of around $1.1 million in 2000 to 2002, then declined by 44 percent between 2003 and 2005 after the tech market crash and the Global Settlement. (See Exhibit 2.8.) The study shows that dramatic growth in compensation at the firm from 1995 to 2002 was fueled by large real bonus growth rates (averaging 45 percent in 1995, 21 percent in 1996, 33 percent in 1997, and 77 percent in 2000). When the market declined in 2003 and 2005, however, average real bonuses declined by 33 percent and 26 percent respectively.[34]

In contrast to the wide swings in bonuses, *nominal* salaries at the firm grew modestly over time, from an average of $146,667 in 1988 to $173,077 in 2005. However, *nominal* salary growth rates were less than rates of inflation, implying that mean *real* salaries declined from $239,535 in 1988 to $173,077 in 2005.[35]

The large increases in compensation that occurred during the late 1990s were not shared equally among the analysts at the firm. In 2002, analysts in the top decile of the compensation distribution received $3,236,484 (in 2005 dollars), more than three times the compensation of the median analyst (see Exhibit 2.8).[36] Well-known research analysts at the leading firms, such as Henry Blodget, Mary Meeker, and Jack Grubman, earned even larger amounts, with rumored compensation of more than $10 million a year, much of it driven by investment banking awards. Dan Reingold described the compensation package he was offered by Credit Suisse First Boston (CSFB) in 1999:

> Instead of a fixed salary and bonus, CSFB was offering me a piece of the action: 2.5 percent of any telecom [investment banking] fees earned by

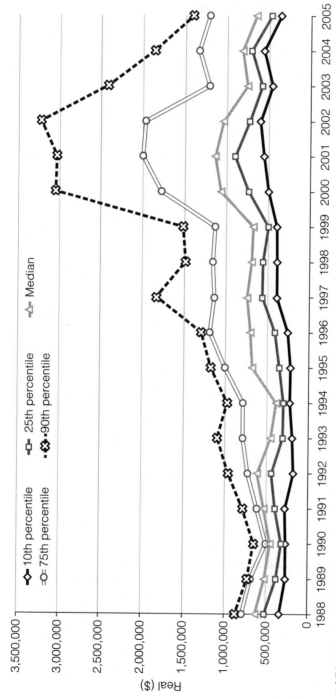

Exhibit 2.8. Distribution of sell-side analysts' total compensation at a leading investment bank from 1988 to 2005 (in 2005 dollars). The sample comprised 609 analyst-year observations, with analysts per year ranging from twenty-six to forty-two. Total compensation equals salary plus bonus. Compensation data were inflation adjusted using CPI data from the Federal Reserve Economic Database (FRED).

SOURCE: Groysberg, B., P. Healy, and D. Maber. 2011. What drives sell-side analyst compensation at high-status investment banks? *Journal of Accounting Research* 49: 969–1000.

CSFB above $150 million per year . . . There were also payments for an *II* ranking of number one, two, or three and additional incentives if CSFB ranked in the top five spots in three different league tables: telecom M&A, telecom stock underwriting, and telecom junk-bond underwriting.[37]

By the late 1990s, the bulk of analysts were earning a half a million, and highly ranked analysts were earning a couple of million dollars a year. However, by 2005, these mega-deals had disappeared, and analyst pay inequality declined.

Groysberg, Healy, and Maber (2011) find that differences in analysts' total compensation can be largely explained by three factors: institutional client ratings of analysts, coverage of the firm's investment banking clients, and the aggregate trading volume of the stocks the analyst covers. Analysts at the firm with a top three or runner-up rating in *Institutional Investor* received 61 percent (100 percent) higher total (bonus) compensation than their unranked peers. Analysts who covered a current investment banking client earned 8 percent (12 percent) higher total (bonus) compensation. And analysts who covered stocks at the third trading volume quartile earned 48 percent (64 percent) higher total (bonus) compensation than analysts at the first trading volume quartile, reflecting the importance of having strong analysts covering stocks that have a disproportionate impact on business.[38]

Conclusions

As capital market intermediaries, sell-side analysts provide research ideas to buy-side investors and help create an informed, liquid, and orderly market for stocks. To perform this function, analysts have to have a deep knowledge and understanding of the industries and firms they cover, build a loyal clientele for their services by marketing and refining their ideas with clients, and leverage their time by collaborating with junior research analysts, the institutional sales force, and traders within their own firms.

To manage sell-side research successfully, sell-side firms hire analysts who have strong intellectual, work ethic, entrepreneurial, risk-taking, and communication skills. Hiring strategies vary across firms, with some hiring established star analysts from other firms and others hiring rookies with the goal of developing them into stars. Research managers provide analysts with training and mentoring to help them build their franchise, particularly for firms that develop talent internally rather than hiring stars. Finally, research departments spend considerable time and resources evaluating analyst performance and determining analyst compensation.

3

Sell-Side Research:
The History of an Information Good

In Chapter 1 we discussed the challenges Prudential faced in monetizing sell-side research. In this chapter we argue that this challenge arises because sell-side research is an "information good," which affects its value to customers.

Information Good Problems

Financial services firms fund and support research departments because they anticipate that sell-side research attracts clients and contributes to their profitability. However, as an information product, research faces a number of challenges that influence not only its value to customers but their willingness to pay for the product. These include (1) high costs of information production and low costs of reproduction; (2) rapid information obsolescence in an efficient capital market; (3) "experience good" attributes; and (4) information overload.

Cost of Production versus Reproduction

Although the initial cost of producing research is high, its cost of reproduction or redistribution is very low. The initial production costs include analysts' salaries, their administrative support costs, travel expenses, office space, and the other infrastructure costs of supporting research. However, once these costs have been incurred, the incremental costs of research distribution are very low, particularly now that research findings can be distributed via the Internet. As a result, the cost of the first research report is very high, but each additional report that is distributed costs virtually nothing.

From a business perspective this characteristic can create challenges in pricing and profitability. Because the up-front initial production costs are sunk, competing research providers have incentives to lower prices to attract new clients and cover their production costs—after all, any price greater than the cost of reproduction makes a positive contribution. The resulting pricing pressure can lead all firms in the industry to suffer from low profitability and makes it a challenge to cover the full cost of research production. This problem is not unique to equity research—it is also faced by the software and music industries. Later in this chapter we explore how sell-side research has been packaged and sold to mitigate this risk. Initially the industry bundled research with trade execution and sold the package to customers at regulated prices. Later, when prices were deregulated, research was bundled with investment banking.

Information Obsolescence

Another important feature of research is that its value depends in part on the number of other clients who have access to it. If financial markets are relatively efficient, new research findings will be quickly reflected in prices as customers trade on the information uncovered by analysts. However, this implies that the information is valuable only to clients who are able to react quickly to new information the analyst provides. Clients who are slower to respond will find that the information has become obsolete and cannot help them generate superior returns. As a result, the information is very valuable to the clients who either receive the information first or who are able to react to it promptly. But it is virtually worthless to clients who react slowly.

This feature of equity research further complicates pricing and profitability. U.S. securities regulations require financial institutions that produce research to provide it to all clients at the same time. Consequently, research providers cannot issue their reports earlier to some clients than to others and charge differentially. However, as we discuss later in this chapter, research providers have figured out ways to allow clients who valued information in their analysts' research reports to compensate them differentially for the research.

Of course, if markets are not perfectly efficient, or if portfolio managers have diverse views on a stock, even research that has been widely distributed may have some value to research users. In addition, portfolio managers may be willing to pay for basic research on a stock even if it does not enable them to generate superior returns. It is much more efficient for the thousands of money management firms and portfolio managers to acquire basic information on stocks from a handful of sell-side firms than to incur the costs of replicating this information internally.

Research as an Experience Good

A good is an "experience good" if consumers have to use it to be able to value it. Consumers of such a product or service bear a risk that it will not live up to their expectations once they have purchased and experienced it. This reduces their willingness to make the purchase in the first place and/or leads them to require a price discount to protect against the risk.

Many goods and services—music, movies, software, new products—qualify as experience goods because it is difficult to assess how entertaining or useful they are until one has actually listened to the music, watched the movie, or used the software or new product. Equity research is also an experience good. Portfolio managers do not know whether a new research idea will provide any useful information until they have actually received it. Even then, an idea's value is not evident. An analyst can predict whether a stock will increase or decrease in value, usually over the next twelve months, but the value of that prediction becomes evident only with the passage of time. This creates an additional risk for the clients of sell-side departments and therefore for research providers in pricing their product.

As discussed later in this chapter, research firms use several approaches to mitigate this challenge. It is partially overcome through branding and reputation—portfolio managers value the research of a particular firm or analyst they have used in the past and found valuable. It is also managed through the system of broker votes used to allocate commissions, where buy-side analysts and portfolio managers rate the value of past sell-side research for analysts and their firms and use the ratings as a basis for assigning future commissions.

Information Overload

An increasingly important challenge for producers and users of research is that voluminous information is available at so little cost, leading to information overload. This is certainly true for many stocks where a wealth of information is available from the financial media, online investment advisors, and sell-side analysts, as well as from the company itself. It is thus challenging for portfolio managers to screen all the new information potentially available on a stock and judge its reliability.

Once again, we argue that branding and reputation of sell-side analysts and research departments play an important role in helping the buy-side perform these functions. Independent ratings of analysts by organizations such as *Institutional Investor* and Greenwich Associates also provide investors with a way to determine which analysts are worth listening to and which are not.

These properties of equity research raise challenges for research producers in pricing and profitability. Yet, as we discuss next, for much of its history the industry has managed to develop business models to mitigate these effects.

Sell-Side Research and the Brokerage Business Model

The first research department was created in 1926 by Edward Shearson, who hired Murray Safanie, an accountant working at the U.S. Treasury Department, and charged him with providing clients at Shearson's brokerage firm with "as much factual information as possible on the stocks they bought and sold."[1]

Yet it was not until 1959 that research developed into a business. At that time, William Donaldson, Daniel Lufkin, and Richard Jenrette, former Harvard Business School classmates, recognized the unique opportunity provided by rapidly growing pension funds and mutual funds that were increasingly looking for ideas on how to outperform the market. The firm they created, Donaldson, Lufkin & Jenrette (DLJ), had a novel business model: Fill the "information void"[2] by providing institutional investors with well-researched investment ideas, and they will reward you handsomely with brokerage business and, thus, commission dollars. In the words of Jack Rivkin, who started in the industry as a sell-side analyst in 1968 and later became a research director, "People were doing research long before DLJ, but [DLJ] made it into a business."[3]

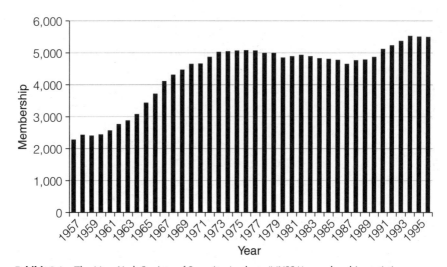

Exhibit 3.1. The New York Society of Security Analysts (NYSSA) membership statistics.

SOURCE: Authors, from data in Timothy C. Jacobson, From Practice to Profession: A History of the Financial Analysts Federation and the Investment Profession, Association for Investment Management and Research (1997), CFA Institute Web page, www.cfainstitute.org/aboutus/press/60thanniversary/index.html, retrieved in June 2008, p. 24.

When DLJ became the first New York Stock Exchange member to go public in 1970, the firm was earning a return on equity of more than 50 percent, and many others had copied their business model. Faulkner, Oppenheimer and Dawkins & Sullivan were formed in the early 1960s, followed by Sanford C. Bernstein & Co. in 1967. With dozens of firms providing equity research, the industry had come of age.

The profession grew from fewer than 2,500 analysts (both buy- and sell-side analysts) in 1957 to more than 5,000 in 1975 (see Exhibit 3.1). Analysts with backgrounds in industry and academia were encouraged to join the sell-side, bringing expertise and specialization.

Regulated Commissions

The early success of the industry depended largely on the fact that research was funded through regulated commissions. Institutional commissions on the NYSE were a direct function of both price and shares traded:

$$\text{Commission per share} = \alpha + \beta \times \text{Price}$$

The coefficients α and β varied with trade size, and commissions on trades above \$300,000 could be negotiated. But brokers were prohibited from competing for clients by offering lower-priced commissions. Instead they offered auxiliary services such as research. Thus, when a buy-side house (for example, an investment firm such as Fidelity) executed a trade with a broker, they would pay that broker a commission of twenty to thirty cents per share. The buy-side house would also advise the broker what, if any, sell-side research led to the trade. The broker would then write a "give-up" check to the research firm, often specifying the analysts who had contributed to the deal. Research firms, in one veteran analyst's words, were "service organizations that relied upon fees."

Regulated commissions enabled research firms to overcome many of the information good problems discussed earlier in this chapter. By prohibiting brokers from competing by cutting commissions, they ensured that sell-side analysts and firms were rewarded for their work and remained profitable. This allowed the sell-side research profession to attract new talent, notably graduates from leading colleges and new analysts who had industry experience.

As a result, research became more sophisticated. Analysts were encouraged to spend much of their time in the field. Robert B. Johnson (then director of research at Paine, Webber, Jackson & Curtis) indicated that his team spent as much as 50 to 70 percent of their time traveling, visiting the management of institutions and corporations.[4] In addition, the simplistic relationship-based advice of the 1950s, often conducted via telephone or wire service, was replaced by in-depth reports on a particular company or industry. As one veteran analyst puts it, such reports were "magnificent . . . documents," perhaps more than 150 pages on one company, elegantly hardbound and typeset.

Firms sought to build strong research brands to differentiate themselves, reducing the "experience good" risk and the "information overload" challenges for their clients. For example, Daniel Lufkin came up with the initial idea of "producing in-depth research reports on small companies, patterned after the analyses of case studies he had done at Harvard."[5] Analysts at Sanford C. Bernstein became well known for the depth of their analysis, the length of their reports or "Black Books," and a focus on long-term forecasts of a company's prospects. As one Bernstein veteran put it, "We're not trying to give you a weather forecast. We're trying to tell you whether there's going to be a heat wave or an ice age."[6] As a result of such efforts, money managers could readily identify the most reliable sources of information on particular companies and could have confidence that the reports they received met their expectations. As James Balog recalls fondly, the era "was a Camelot period in the research business."[7]

Deregulation and Consolidation

By the early 1970s, commissions were twenty to thirty cents per share. Yet on May 1, 1975, termed "May Day" on Wall Street, the U.S. Securities Exchange Commission deregulated the brokerage industry by abolishing regulated high fixed commission rates and permitting commissions to be determined by market competition. Consequently, numerous brokerage firms were forced to modify the funding structure of their equity research departments. Research and brokerage firms demanded hard dollars for research materials and began to charge steep fees for individual reports or annual subscriptions. Morgan Stanley, for example, charged $500 for a short ten-page report, between $5,000 and $7,000 annually for all research in a particular industry, and more than $25,000 annually for comprehensive access to the firm's research.[8] Paine Webber followed suit.

The impact of the regulatory changes on individual analysts was dramatic. Robert Errigo, former research director at Merrill Lynch, explains, "The analyst went from being an intellectual introvert to becoming a dominant salesperson of his research. Analysts who couldn't sell were driven out of business."[9] Other analysts remarked that scholarly aspects of their profession declined; the focus, they felt, shifted from detailed book-like reports to stock-picking abilities.

In addition to the job changes, analysts saw their compensation decline by 10 to 12 percent. Top analysts retained their jobs and high compensation, but others either lost their jobs or settled for less money as a two-tier market developed. In 1977, most Street analysts earned between $40,000 and $50,000; the biggest names earned as much as $125,000.[10]

The changes that May Day brought, however, did not stop with the intellectual focus and compensation of research analysts. Deregulation had a profound effect on the structure of the industry. Commission rates for institutional trades declined dramatically. Rates for blocks of 1,000 to 9,999 shares fell from 27.6 cents per share in April 1975 to close to 15 cents in December 1978, and rates for orders of 10,000 or more also fell during the same period. (See Exhibit 3.2.)

Security firms that focused on institutional clients struggled to break even, leading to consolidation and dissolution. The total number of firms

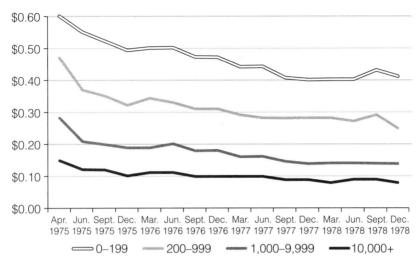

Exhibit 3.2. Commission rates for institutions by order size, April 1975 to December 1978.
SOURCE: Securities and Exchange Commission, Survey of Commission Charges on Brokerage Transactions, July 26, 1979, p. 13.

on the *Institutional Investor* All-America ranking in 1974 was sixty-one; by 1981 that number had shrunk to twenty-five. H. C. Wainwright, the number-one research firm in 1974, folded; seven of the top ten firms were no longer around or survived only through a merger. These included Mitchell Hutchins, the number-three firm in 1974, Drexel Burnham (ranked fourth), William D. Witter (fifth), G. H. Walker Laird (eighth), Baker Weeks (ninth), and Colemen (tenth). Only three firms emerged from the 1970s unscathed: DLJ, Morgan Stanley, and Oppenheimer.[11]

Whether tragic or necessary, May Day changed the face of Wall Street and the features of equity research in particular. As practitioners sought novel ways to get paid, the profession began to reinvent itself. Under the new model, most analysts were affiliated with large investment banks.

Research and Investment Banking

By the early 1980s, the outlook for sell-side research was finally looking up. As *Institutional Investor* put it at the time:

Today, the environment for Wall Street research appears healthy once again. The shakeout in the industry seems to have ceased; organizations have scrambled to their feet again and are only too eager to build up their research efforts. And analysts are being tempted with the kinds of salary offers they suspected were gone forever.[12]

However, as *Institutional Investor* pointed out, the nature of analysts' work changed markedly during this period:

> Analysts are expected to spend ever-greater portions of their time marketing their products to institutions and contributing to other areas of their firms, leaving fewer hours for research.[13]

Rising to meet these demands often required collaboration, leading to team structures that gained popularity in other areas of the brokerage firm.

The reemergence of equity research arose from a change in the business model, as firms with investment banking departments recognized that their equity research departments could be used to leverage corporate underwriting. Sell-side analysts were valued because their sales and marketing skills and their connections with leading institutional investors could help the bankers distribute new offerings. In addition, the analysts could help to generate corporate finance deals. Leading analysts had close relations with managers of issuer firms and could often anticipate which were likely to be good candidates for banking services. Corporate issuer managers perceived that the leading analysts had influence with the investing community and could help generate interest in their stock during the period following an issue. Banks that had no analyst covering an issuer were increasingly excluded from the deal.

As a result of the synergies between research and investment banking, a new model for funding research emerged. Research departments continued to be cost centers at their firms, partially funded by contributions from deregulated brokerage commissions. But now an increasing source of funds came from allocations via the investment banking department. For example, in the early 1990s, analysts estimated that Goldman Sachs spent $105 million per annum on research, and Merrill Lynch $125 million.[14] By the late 1990s, research spending at the largest firms had risen to over $500 million per annum, with a disproportionate share of the increase funded by investment banking business. In 2000, roughly 42 percent of equity research department budgets at leading banks was paid for by investment banking,[15] up from around 15 percent in the early 1990s.[16]

In addition to direct support for research departments, investment banking departments provided lucrative end-of-year bonuses to financial analysts who contributed to their profits. A recent paper by Groysberg,

Healy, and Maber (2011) reports that during the period from 1988 to 2005, analysts at a leading bank who helped generate $1 million or more in banking-related revenue earned 7 percent more compensation than peers who had no banking contributions.

The rise of investment banking funding of research enabled the industry to grow rapidly throughout the 1990s. The number of senior equity analysts almost doubled between 1992 and 1999. From 1992 to 1998, Merrill Lynch consistently employed the largest number of equity analysts. Merrill analysts also produced the most company reports (two pages or longer)—12,470 for 4,504 companies in 1998, compared to 4,198 for Credit Suisse First Boston, which was a distant second.[17]

By using investment banking fees to support research, financial institutions were able to overcome many of the information good challenges discussed earlier in this chapter. Because corporate issuers valued the ability of sell-side analysts to help market their stock during an IPO or seasoned issue and to facilitate market liquidity following an issue by providing investors with continuous information on the stock, they were willing to pay for research services through investment banking fees. From the investment bank's perspective, their research departments contributed to their overall profitability, even though they were typically treated as cost centers.

Superstar Analysts and Rankings

In the late 1990s, veteran telecommunications analyst Jack Grubman became one of the first analysts to rise to celebrity status. He received a one-year $25 million compensation package from Salomon Smith Barney.[18] Some firms found themselves offering packages to star analysts that were significantly more than their entire research budgets a decade before. In 1998 recruiters noted that the average compensation for ranked analysts had tripled within the past few years. Susan Decker, head of equity research at DLJ, believed that compensation levels had risen 300 percent for the top equity analysts over the past five years.[19] Star analysts who covered industries such as telecommunications, technology, media, and health care could expect to be paid $2 million to $5 million through a combination of salary, bonuses, stocks, and options. Second-tier analysts earned from $750,000 to $1 million, and junior analysts received from $500,000 to $750,000. The so-called grunts, whose work backed up the senior analysts, could be paid as much as $250,000 to $400,000.[20]

How did an analyst achieve superstar status and the compensation to go with it? *Institutional Investor* published the first ranking of sell-side equity analysts in its October 1972 issue. The ranking was based on a survey of approximately 300 buy-side institutions that accounted for 75 to 80 percent of U.S. equity commissions. Buy-side analysts and portfolio managers were asked to vote for the best analysts in twenty-six sectors. The names of the top vote getters across these sectors, eighty-five analysts in total, were featured in *Institutional Investor* as the "All-America Research Team." Most sectors had three winning analysts with one to three runners-up.

Over the years, *Institutional Investor* made a number of refinements to its annual survey. In 1973, the sector winners were divided into first-, second-, and third-place finishers (referred to as first teamers, second teamers, and third teamers) and runners-up. In 1974, a "Leaders Table" was added that ranked sell-side firms by the number of analysts who had achieved an *Institutional Investor* ranking. This ranking was later adjusted with the results weighted based on whether analysts earned a first, second, third, or runner-up position.

The industries covered changed over time, and by 2011 sixty-five industries were included in the ranking. In 1977, a second firm leaderboard was added that ranked firms based on the percentage of their analysts who achieved an *Institutional Investor* ranking.

In the late 1970s, Greenwich Associates ("Greenwich") launched a competitive poll that asked buy-side investors to rank their top sell-side research firms. While *Institutional Investor* mailed its survey to a large number of investment professionals at buy-side firms, Greenwich obtained its results via in-depth interviews with buy-side firm managers and senior personnel. Greenwich did not make the results of its survey freely available but rather limited its dissemination to paying clients.

In 1985, *Institutional Investor* expanded its survey, asking buy-side respondents to score analysts on a scale of one to ten across a number of categories, including stock picking, earnings estimates and client service.[21] What factors were considered important to institutional investors in their ratings of sell-side analysts? In 1998, analysts' understanding of the industry they covered was rated the number-one factor regardless of institution size.[22] For the largest clients this was followed by stock selection, written reports, and company visits. However, these rankings changed over time.

By 1998, the ranking surveyed roughly 1,800 portfolio managers who represented approximately 88 percent of the 100 largest U.S. equity managers, as well as nearly 300 other investment management institutions, banks, money managers, and investment counseling firms. Because the *Institutional Investor* rankings reflected what customers valued most in analysts,[23] they were considered a more comprehensive indicator of an analyst's performance than the performance of stock recommendations and/or earnings forecasts. *Institutional Investor* became the industry standard and was used as a hiring and evaluation tool by firms, as a basis for pay negotiations by analysts, and as a marketing tool by investment bankers. Being ranked by *Institutional Investor* made an analyst tremendously powerful on Wall Street, and ranked analysts were generally referred to as star analysts. Brokerage firms often advertised their ranked analysts in newspapers, including taking out full-page ads boasting of their "first team" winners. Newspapers and television outlets sought opinions from *Institutional Investor* analysts on the best and worst stocks.

Institutional Investor rankings helped issuers to quickly identify who were the key analysts covering their stocks, facilitating the selection of investment banks that were well equipped to underwrite or help distribute new offerings. The rankings also helped money managers identify the highest-valued research departments and analysts. By building relationships with these analysts and assigning brokerage business to their firms, money managers could anticipate an increased likelihood of being allocated shares in attractive (rationed) new issues.

Brokerage Commission Funding Revisited

Although investment banking emerged as a dominant source of research funding during the 1980s and 1990s, brokerage funding continued to be important. Indeed, some firms, such as Sanford C. Bernstein, chose not to develop investment banking capabilities and relied exclusively on brokerage commissions to support their research.

One reason for the ongoing role of brokerage funding was that institutional investors continued to demand fundamental research on stocks. Despite lower costs of information collection and the growth of buy-side research departments, sell-side research provided a very efficient way for institutional investors and hedge funds to purchase fundamental research on industry economics and firm strategy and to use the sell-side's ability to provide efficient access to corporate managers.

Of course, for brokerage firms that relied heavily on brokerage commissions to fund research, the challenges confronting information goods discussed earlier in this chapter remained. And, with deregulation, brokerage rates declined precipitously. These challenges were somewhat offset by the rise of analyst rankings and broker votes.

Analyst Ratings

The growth of analyst and research department rankings described in the preceding pages helped money managers cope with information overload. Analyst rankings enabled money managers to identify the leading analysts covering stocks of interest and to focus primarily on their research reports, rather than sifting through potentially dozens of reports from unranked analysts.

Analyst reputations generated from rankings by *Institutional Investor* (or Greenwich Associates) were also useful for money managers in limiting experience good risk. The ratings signified that buy-side peers found the star analyst's research to be valuable. Although a strong rating did not eliminate the possibility that a star analyst's future research would be less valuable, the stickiness in the ratings provided money managers with some assurance that the value would persist.

Client or Broker Votes

Sell-side analysts are also regularly rated by managers of large money management firms as a way of allocating their firms' trading. At these annual or semiannual votes, buy-side analysts and portfolio managers receive a number of votes to allocate to sell-side analysts based on the relative value of their research advice and services received. Trading volume over the next six to twelve months is then allocated to firms in proportion to their votes. As one buy-side analyst described the process:

> We sit down twice a year and think about what we've done over the last six months, and about which sell-side analysts have been most helpful. And then we each allocate a fixed number of points. I have to allocate my points across the sell-side firms and analysts, and they get paid a certain dollar amount [in the form of future trade commission] based on the allocation of those points.

While the format differs by firm, most asset managers conduct a broker vote and then communicate the results of the vote to research department managers. Buy-side firms generally break down the votes received by a sell-side firm by analyst and even by service (for example, written research, analyst visits, company management visits). Some firms also break down the total commissions paid into two categories: how much they are paying for trade execution and how much they are paying for other services, such as research.

By linking money managers' trading decisions with their ex post assessments of sell-side research quality, the broker votes system reduces the risk associated with experience goods. Money managers get to experience whether particular research and analyst interactions add value before they determine how to allocate payments to investment banks and brokerage firms for their research in the form of trading commissions. The method also provides sell-side research departments with useful information for judging and rewarding sell-side analysts' performance.

Despite the potential benefits provided by analyst ratings and client votes, sell-side firms that relied exclusively on brokerage commissions to fund research struggled to retain their most talented analysts during the 1980s and 1990s. Investment banks were able to offer their star analysts considerably higher compensation for their services. Some star analysts at these firms earned less and left for higher-paying jobs at investment banks.

Conclusions

It would be costly and inefficient for the thousands of institutional investors that utilize sell-side research to replicate it using their own resources. Yet sell-side research departments have faced a challenge in selling their services at prices that cover the cost of initial production. One explanation for this paradox is that sell-side research is an information good with characteristics that make it challenging for research departments to monetize their product. In a competitive industry, because the costs of reproducing research are low there is downward pressure on rates of reimbursement for research. Research information can quickly become obsolete. As an experience good, clients find it difficult to evaluate the quality of research ideas until they have received and acted on them. And clients face information overload and challenges in screening and evaluating the quality of research.

Yet the industry has been remarkably adaptive over the years in devising ways to overcome these limitations. Early in its history the industry saw that it could bundle research with trade execution and recover its costs through regulated brokerage commissions that constrained firms' incentives to discount their research. In addition, the creation of client ratings reduced costs of information overload for investors, and money manager voting systems that linked their feedback on sell-side research to their firms' subsequent allocation of brokerage business mitigated the experience good and information obsolescence problems of sell-side research.

When commission rates were deregulated in 1975, research firms quickly recognized that they would have to follow a different path to cover the costs of research. Many saw that corporate issuers valued the role that research played in selling new issues and making a liquid market for their stocks. Issuers were therefore willing to help cover the cost of sell-side research through investment banking fees. Institutional investor ratings of sell-side analysts provided issuer firm managers with an easy way to identify the most influential analysts, leading these analysts to become increasingly valuable to investment bankers. The leading analysts became stars in the business media, developed close relations with managers of the firms they covered, and were paid handsomely. However, as we saw in Chapter 1 for Prudential and discuss later, this system led to excesses and concern about conflicts of interest. The resulting regulation has once again transformed the industry.

4

Investment Banking Model Challenges

The investment banking model used to fund research and to create star analysts during the 1990s successfully supported the growing number of new equity issues in the Internet and telecommunications industries. However, as the model rose in prominence, so too did concerns about analyst independence and conflicts of interest. Reflecting this concern, in December 2000, when Prudential announced it was drastically downsizing its investment banking operations, Prudential CEO John Strangfeld stated, "We expect this strategic change to make Prudential Securities the first major Wall Street securities firm to use its research capability to primarily serve its individual and institutional investors rather than its investment bank."[1] In this chapter we discuss challenges to the investment banking model that have emerged during the last fifteen years, primarily in the form of new regulations that have limited banks' ability to use investment banking to monetize sell-side research.

Conflicts of Interest and Investment Banking

During the 1990s, research budgets grew rapidly, funded largely by investment banking. Investment banking departments funded research in two ways. First, in the annual budget negotiations, they agreed to support a certain share of the research budget. In addition, at year-end, investment banking departments awarded significant bonuses to analysts who helped to attract new underwriting business and market new issues to investors. For example, Henry Blodget, a highly ranked technology analyst at Merrill Lynch, was paid $12 million in 2001. A 1999 memo showed that he spent 85 percent of his time on investment banking activities and 15 percent on research-related activities.[2] Another memo, written in 2000, indicated that his team had worked on more than fifty-two investment banking deals that had generated more than $115 million in fees for Merrill Lynch.[3]

The substantial bonus awards paid to superstar analysts such as Blodget, Mary Meeker, and Jack Grubman, who supported their firms' investment banking business during the boom in Internet and telecommunications stock issues, generated concern over conflicts of interest between sell-side research and investment banking. One industry veteran observed that the analyst's role changed dramatically during this period. In the 1970s, an analyst wouldn't even get on the same elevator with an investment banker for fear that people would think the two had exchanged client or market information. But by the 1990s, those days were long gone, and Wall Street insiders began to view the modern analyst as "an investment banker in sheep's clothing."[4]

Of course, many analysts recognized that their long-term success depended on being viewed as independent from investment banking. For example, Michael Culp, ex-director of research at Prudential-Bache Securities Inc., explained that when an analyst was "viewed as a mouthpiece for investment banking, their career is over. . . . The best mark of an analyst is having two managements that want you dead."[5] Another industry veteran, Barry Tarasoff, director of research at Wertheim Schroder & Co, emphasized that "the toughest part of the job is to maintain the integrity of the research—and unless the organization understands the importance of that integrity at the highest level, it's doubly hard."[6]

Yet, in reality, investment banking revenues were important for the banks and a critical source of support for research departments; issuer companies weren't afraid to exploit that fact. In one high-profile case, Conseco fired Merrill Lynch as its lead underwriter on a newly announced $325 million convertible-bond offering and stopped dealing with Merrill for about two weeks after Edward Spehar, who covered life insurer stocks at Merrill, downgraded Conseco's stock to a buy from a strong buy.[7] While Conseco's management claimed that the firing of Merrill Lynch was unrelated to the analyst's "unfavorable" comments, insiders claimed that Conseco Chairman Stephen Hilbert phoned to fire Merrill Lynch shortly after the downgrade and that the two events were linked. In August of 1995, just a week after Spehar left Merrill Lynch for Lehman Brothers, Conseco returned to Merrill to underwrite an initial public offering of 15 million common shares of American Life Group Inc. Ironically, Merrill replaced Spehar with Salomon Brothers Inc.'s analyst, who also rated Conseco's stock a buy. Perrin Long, a securities industry analyst at Brown Brothers Harriman, explained the dilemma such a case demonstrated: "Do they want to give up the corporation or do they want to retain the fees and give up the analyst?"[8]

The risks to analyst independence were further demonstrated by Janney Montgomery Scott's decision to fire its analyst Marvin Roffman for questioning the financial stability of Donald Trump's casino empire after Trump threatened a major lawsuit.[9] Jack Rivkin, a research director at Lehman at that time, immediately wrote a letter to *The Wall Street Journal* blaming Janney Montgomery Scott for its action. In his letter Rivkin wrote, "I could understand firing Mr. Roffman next February, after the cold winds had blown and he proved to be wrong. That is a risk all analysts run. But he was fired for putting forth an opinion."[10]

The SEC and the House subcommittee that oversaw the SEC both decided to investigate the firing and concluded that it raised "serious public policy issues."[11] The analyst's main trade association, the Association for Investment Management and Research, issued a press release arguing that "the right of the investment public to receive objective investment advice is dependent on the analyst being able to communicate judgments without coercion or fear of reprisal."[12]

In the end, the analyst's report turned out to be correct, as Trump ran into financial difficulties. One analyst concluded:

> The problem lies not with the Donald Trumps of the world. The objectivity and independence of the analyst community steadily eroded during the 1980s as analysts abandoned primary research to pursue trading volume and investment banking fees. It is little wonder that we are where we are.[13]

Impact on Recommendations

The tremendous pressure on analysts to make positive recommendations was reflected in the relatively low frequency of negative recommendations issued. The percentage of sell-side recommendations troughed in the late 1990s, during the height of the investment banking model, and has risen marginally since. A 1990 study of Wall Street recommendations on 1,500 companies showed that 44.6 percent were buys or strong buys, and 45.6 percent were holds. Only 9.7 percent were sells or strong sells.[14] By 1998, according to Zacks Investment Research, only 1.4 percent of all analysts' recommendations on about 6,000 companies were sells compared to 31.1 percent holds and 67.5 percent buys.[15] According to Thomson Financial, in 2002 nearly 70 percent of U.S. stocks were rated buy, and only 2.5 percent were sell recommendations.[16] By late 2008, the percentage of stocks rated sell had risen to 6.7 percent, with 48.6 percent of stocks rated buy.[17]

There are a number of explanations for the scarcity of negative stock recommendations. First, companies often react negatively to being told they are rated a sell. As a senior equity analyst described, "It was awful having to pick up the phone to talk to companies because they didn't like talking to you. They treat you differently. They don't like it. It's bad news." As analysts rely heavily on access to company management to conduct their research, this can be problematic. Second, buy-side clients do not like to see a stock they own rated sell, particularly if they bought the stock on that analyst's prior recommendation. As an analyst at Bernstein asserted, "To make the right recommendation change as an analyst, you have to downgrade the stock just when everyone is loving it! When you do that, what tends to happen is that clients hate you." Additionally, other divisions within analyst firms may find their relationships with clients damaged if an analyst puts a sell recommendation on a stock. Investment bankers trying to win a secondary equity issuance from a company, for example, would find their job more difficult if one of their own analysts has rated the company a sell. Finally, historically, most sell-side clients were long-only investors, and as such they were focused primarily on buy ideas. As a result, professional investors have come to view a hold recommendation as effectively equivalent to a sell. Dan Reingold, a former telecom analyst, explained:

> Sell ratings offer little payoff to a Wall Street analyst. This is because, for the most part, institutional investors are paid to pick stocks that go up . . . If a stock falls or performs in line with the market, the Wall Street analyst who rated that stock a Hold or Neutral looks almost as good to his clients as the one who rated it Sell. As a result, analysts didn't have much incentive to go out on a limb with a much riskier Sell rating, even before banking pressures emerged.[18]

Wall Street Journal's John R. Dorfman explained that the hold recommendation "is a notorious euphemism on Wall Street. Many firms use the word to mean 'We'd sell this turkey if we were you, but we don't want to come right out and say so because we might offend the company or lose its investment banking business.'"[19]

Some money managers dealt with the imbalance in research recommendations by focusing on the direction of analysts' ratings rather than on their one-word opinions. A downgrade from a strong buy to buy could generate heavy selling. More than ever, money managers called analysts directly to get the real story on a stock. Alan Sachtleben, chief equity investment officer at the Chicago-based mutual fund company Van Kampen American Capital, remarked: "If you know an analyst is probably involved in an underwriting, you take that into consideration."[20] Another in the industry summarized:

> I don't think there's an institutional investor who doesn't understand how a large brokerage house or investment bank runs its business. There's not a single investor sitting there under the delusion that analysts are completely independent. Now having said that, I think they're as independent as they can be. And really, that has everything to do with the fact that most analysts have a high level of integrity to realize that they need to be independent in order to keep their own business going. I'm not aware of a single analyst who (a) wanted to, or (b) was ever allowed to change his recommendation because he was trying to increase a piece of business flow. So there's a natural balance in how an analyst runs his business, altogether. But it is the case that if it's a global investment bank that you work for, somebody in that investment bank is probably trying to pitch business to every single company that you cover. So an institutional investor is obviously going to be aware of that when he's looking at recommendations.

The Spitzer Investigation

In 2001, Elliot Spitzer, then attorney general of New York, launched an investigation into the research and underwriting practices of several large investment banks. Spitzer's investigation started with Merrill Lynch, where investigators alleged that:

> Since late 1999, the internet research analysts (the "internet group") at Merrill Lynch have published on a regular basis ratings for internet stocks

that were misleading because: (1) the ratings in many cases did not reflect the analysts' true opinions of the companies; (2) as a matter of undisclosed, internal policy, no "reduce" or "sell" recommendations were issued, thereby converting a published five-point rating scale into a de facto three-point system; and (3) Merrill Lynch failed to disclose to the public that Merrill Lynch's ratings were tarnished by an undisclosed conflict of interest: the research analysts were acting as quasi-investment bankers for the companies at issue, often initiating, continuing, and/or manipulating research coverage for the purpose of attracting and keeping investment banking clients, thereby producing misleading ratings that were neither objective nor independent, as they purported to be.

Behind these ratings was a serious breakdown of the separation between the Merrill Lynch banking and research departments, a separation that was critical to the integrity of the recommendations issued to the public by Merrill Lynch. Though Merrill Lynch's stated policies reflect an understanding that this separation is critical, the evidence reveals that at least with respect to the internet group, there was insufficient divide between research and banking.

Our investigation to date reveals that the compensation system for internet analysts was a significant factor contributing to the breakdown between the internet group and investment banking departments. Research analysts knew that the investment banking business they generated or participated in would impact their compensation, and management encouraged them to produce investment banking business. Analysts curried favor with potential or actual investment banking clients by giving them special treatment. At times, officers of clients or prospective clients were allowed to redraft their own coverage, write quotations in which the analysts would tout their companies, and indicate which rating would be acceptable to them.[21]

As evidence to support these allegations, investigators relied on the well-known paucity of sell recommendations issued by sell-side analysts. The investigation also uncovered evidence of sell-side analysts publishing positive reports on companies they covered, despite privately disparaging the investments. For example, in an e-mail communication, one analyst made derogatory remarks about an Internet company's managers and called the stock "a piece of junk,"[22] yet gave the company, an investment banking client, the firm's highest stock rating. Another expressed concern about giving a buy rating to a poor investment: "I don't think that's the right thing to do . . . John and Mary Smith are losing their retirement because we don't want [GoTo's CFO]'s to be mad at us."[23]

Analyst e-mails also complained about being pressured by their investment banking division. For example, a senior Merrill Lynch analyst wrote, "The whole idea that we are independent of (the) banking (division) is a big lie." Another senior manager stated, "We are off base in how we rate stocks and how much we bend over backwards to accommodate banking."[24]

Research on Investment Banking Conflicts

Despite the compelling email evidence of analyst conflicts uncovered by the New York State attorney general's investigation, it is unclear whether this behavior was pervasive in the industry and how it affected analysts' research. Large sample academic research provides answers to both these questions.

Affiliated Analysts' Forecast and Recommendation Optimism

Several studies have examined whether analysts issue more optimistic earnings forecasts for investment banking clients than for nonbanking clients. One of the first studies on this topic was by Hsiou-wei Lin and Maureen McNichols of Stanford. They examined bias in sell-side analysts forecasts for companies that made seasoned equity offers from 1989 to 1994. They found that the analysts did issue more optimistic long-term earnings growth forecasts for their investment banking clients but reported no such bias in short-term forecasts. On average, analysts whose firms were affiliated with an offer issued long-term growth forecasts of 21.3 percent per year, versus 20.7 percent for analysts from unaffiliated firms.[25] A subsequent study by Patricia Dechow, Amy Hutton, and Richard Sloan, who examined firms issuing new stock from 1981 to 1990, found similar results for short-term forecasts and even larger bias in long-term growth forecasts for affiliated analysts. The mean long-term growth forecasts for their affiliated analysts were 20.1 percent per year versus 15.9 percent for unaffiliated analysts. It is also noteworthy that they reported that both affiliated and unaffiliated analysts' forecasts were wildly optimistic compared to actual annual earnings growth rates for the sample of issue firms for the next five years (which averaged only 5.6 percent).[26]

Academic research has also examined whether affiliated analysts issue more positive stock recommendations than unaffiliated analysts. In their

1998 study, Hsiou-wei Lin and Maureen McNichols reported that 47 percent of affiliated analysts' recommendations were strong buys and 33 percent buys, compared to 37 percent and 24 percent for unaffiliated analysts. In a follow-up 2005 study, Patricia O'Brien, Maureen McNichols, and Hsiou-wei Lin found that analysts were slower to downgrade their recommendations for stocks with bad news that had been investment banking clients than they were for nonbanking clients.[27]

As with any statistical finding, an important caveat is that a *correlation* between two variables, in this case analyst affiliation and research optimism, does not necessarily imply that they are *causally* related. There are two plausible ways to interpret these findings. One is that affiliated analysts bias their research to help investment bankers sell their client's stock. But an equally plausible interpretation is that issuers select investment banks whose analysts are known to have more optimistic opinions on their prospects, thereby facilitating the stock sale.

Stock Market Effects of Affiliated Analyst Optimism

A second important question is whether investors are taken in by affiliated analyst research optimism. If investors are rational, they will anticipate that affiliated analysts are likely to issue optimistic earnings forecasts and recommendations and discount them accordingly. Affiliated analysts' bias should then have little impact on stock prices.

At first blush, the academic evidence seems to indicate that investors are not this rational. New issues are typically underpriced, allowing initial investors to earn strong positive returns on the day of the issue. A well-cited study by Jay Ritter and Ivo Welch, who examine IPOs during the period 1980 to 2001, finds that their average first-day stock return was 18.8 percent. However, market-adjusted returns for the next three years were −23.4 percent, implying that initial investors who "flipped" a stock soon after a new issue earned an attractive short-term gain although subsequent investors faced losses.[28] Could this be attributable to optimistic affiliated analyst research that temporarily misleads investors?

To answer this question, Patricia Dechow, Amy Hutton, and Richard Sloan examine whether post-issue returns for new issue firms are related to optimism in analysts' long-term earnings growth forecasts. Although they find evidence of such a relation, it seems to hold almost equally for forecasts by affiliated and unaffiliated analysts. Hsiou-wei Lin and Maureen McNichols report that investors were more likely to view affiliated analysts' hold recommendations as bad news than those of unaffiliated analysts, suggesting that they recognized that if an affiliated analyst issued a hold recommendation for a banking client, it must really be a poor investment. But they also show that investors did not distinguish between affiliated and unaffiliated analysts' strong buy recommendations. A later study by Michael Cliff and David Denis documents that IPO firms with the highest issue-day returns had a higher frequency of strong buy and buy recommendations from analysts at the lead investment bank.[29] Yet their findings explained only a small fraction of the strong performance of IPOs on issue date.

Overall, this evidence suggests that whatever affiliated optimism does exist, it has only a modest effect on stock prices as investors generally expect affiliate analysts to be biased and factor it into their decisions.

The Global Settlement

In response to the allegations and evidence of analyst wrongdoing collected by the New York State attorney general's office, in October of 2003, ten of the largest investment firms reached an agreement to make changes to their research and investment banking businesses to increase research independence. Within a year, two more firms had joined, for a total of twelve.[30]

The resulting "Global Research Analyst Settlement" amounted to more than $1.4 billion, the largest fine ever assessed on Wall Street firms. Two individual analysts, Jack Grubman of Solomon Smith Barney and Henry Blodget of Merrill Lynch, were fined along with the banks. The Settlement incorporated structural reforms that separated research from investment banking at the involved firms. In all, it covered four major areas: monetary relief, structural reforms, independent research, and investor education.

Monetary Relief

As a part of the final judgment, $417.5 million was to be paid to certain eligible investors through a distribution fund. The Settlement also required the twelve firms to pay out $525 million to the states.

Structural Reforms

Structural reforms required of participating firms comprised the cornerstone of the Settlement.[31] Research and investment banking departments were physically separated to prevent even unintentional flow of information between the two. Compensation of research personnel was to be determined only by research management and the firm's senior management, and a "significant portion" of an analyst's compensation was to be based on quantifiable measures of quality and accuracy. Investment banking was to have no input, and compensation could not be based directly or indirectly on investment banking revenues. These reforms had a dramatic impact on equity research as they essentially removed an important funding source for many firms. Settlement banks now had to look for alternative methods to pay for research. Furthermore, some of the structural reforms affected the whole industry as they were adopted as best practice by banks other than the Settlement banks. As one regulator said in an interview:

> There are some requirements that are only applicable to the settling firms, such as having somebody chaperone a research analyst in their communications with investment bankers. It would be an interesting thing to look at non-Settlement banks and see whether they took some of these as best practices.

Independent Research

One of the most interesting elements of the Settlement was its provision for the purchase of independent research. For a period of five years (beginning July 27, 2004), each firm had to make available to its clients independent research on every company covered by its own research department. An amount of $460 million was designated for this purpose. Each firm was required to hire an independent consultant (IC) to procure the independent research, to monitor its quality over the five-year period, and to submit an annual written report to the regulators. Interestingly, the amount of money each firm was required to set aside to purchase independent research, which ranged from $0.5 million to $15 million per year, was not related to the number of companies covered by its research department or to the number of its retail clients.

Investor Education

The final major component of the Settlement was $80 million set aside for investor education. Of that, $52.5 million was placed into an investor education fund to support programs designed to equip investors with the knowledge and skills necessary to make informed investment decisions.[32]

The remaining $27.5 million was given to state securities regulators to be used for investor education purposes. The Investor Protection Trust (IPT) was designated to govern the fund.

Impact on Research at Investment Banks

The changes imposed by the Settlement had a severe effect on research department budgets at the large investment banks, reducing investment bank funding and analyst head count and compensation and leading to a talent exodus.

Decline in Research Funding

Following the Settlement, the level of research funding contributed by investment banking departments declined dramatically. For example, at Credit Suisse, only 15 percent of equity research department expenses were allocated to the investment banking division's budget in 2008.[33]

As a result, banks reduced head count and cut analyst compensation. A 2003 report by the *Institutional Investor* Research Group stated:

> Cost pressures have forced many formal changes in research department structures and practices: Analyst headcount has been reduced by an average of 15 to 20 percent. And analyst compensation has been trimmed by a third or more. As a result, coverage levels are down by 15 to 25 percent, according to research management.[34]

Industry-wide, the number of sell-side analysts fell from 16,200 in 2000 to 9,300 in 2006.[35] By early 2005, the seven largest Wall Street firms had decreased their spending on equity research by more than 40 percent as compared to 2000 levels.[36]

Between 2000 and 2005, it is estimated that on average senior analyst compensation fell by 50 percent to $750,000[37] While analysts at all levels saw pay decreases, the high end of the pay spectrum was hit the hardest. As previously discussed, star analysts such as Jack Grubman commanded annual compensation packages of up to $20 million or more in the late 1990s.[38] In return, Grubman and other stars were expected to attract and support lucrative investment banking business for their firms. The Global Settlement changed this model, and, as one former research department director pointedly noted, "The economics of the business just doesn't really support star analysts anymore."

Of course, the decision to reduce head count and sell-side compensation undoubtedly reflected a multitude of factors. The stock market was down, and the hot IPO market of the 1990s had burst. When bulge-bracket firms are under pressure to reduce costs, research is often seen as an easy target, viewed as "nice to have, not a need to have" as one buy-side manager puts it. Additionally, the revenue impact of reducing research department expenses is usually lagged, making profitability look artificially high in the near term. A research department manager explained, "When you fire an analyst, revenues do not decrease immediately. First, the [buy-side] votes have to come down, and then the actual payments come down." These considerations surely exacerbated the impact of the Global Settlement and the resulting loss of investment banking revenues.

Talent Exodus

With fewer support resources, increased regulation, and lower compensation, many saw the sell side as a less attractive place to work, reducing the ability of banks to hire and retain top talent. As Harris Hall, director of equity research at Singular Research, opined, "It's such a tough road on the sell-side—analysts are leaving left and right . . . The people staying are carrying heavier workloads, and they're getting paid less. It's not glamorous anymore, it's not lucrative and it's not rewarding."[39] *Institutional Investor* magazine concurred:

> The effects of these measures—including rules that attempt to wall off research departments from the investment banking units of big firms, and limit what CEOs can tell analysts—are still rippling throughout Wall Street, taking much of the fun, money and prestige out of the job of analyzing stocks.[40]

A number of sell-side researchers joined the buy-side or hedge funds. As one buy-side manager stated, "Wall Street does not compensate better analysts the way they used to. Analysts can make more on the buy-side which has led to a talent drain." For example, Barton Biggs, Morgan Stanley's chief strategist, left in 2003 to start a hedge fund, as did Bear Stearns's lodging and gaming analyst, Jason Ader. Mark Alpert, a financial analyst with Deutsche Bank, and Steven Tighe, a drug analyst with Merrill Lynch, both left to join hedge funds. This prompted some industry observers to speculate that sell-side research was becoming a training ground for the buy side.

Many of the industry's most experienced analysts also opted to leave sell-side research for a range of other industries. For example, Tom Berquist, a former Citigroup software analyst, left in March 2006 to become CEO of Ingres Corp., citing increased regulation as one of the key reasons for his move. "If you wanted to have a discussion about a transaction, you had to have lawyers present . . . I miss that contact with all the innovation leaders."[41] Chuck Phillips, a software analyst at Morgan Stanley, left the company to join Oracle Corp., telling friends, "This just isn't fun anymore."[42] In summing up these moves, Richard Leggett, president and CEO of the Center for Financial Research and Analysts, commented that "talent-wise, there's been a significant exodus, the average experience of analysts has declined and the sell-side product is viewed as a commodity."[43]

Decline in Research Quality

The exodus of sell-side talent at the leading banks caused many buy-side investors to complain that the quality of sell-side research has declined materially in recent years. This takes two forms, a decline in coverage and a decline in the quality of current research analysts.

The cuts in research reduced coverage for many stocks. According to Reuters, 17 percent of listed U.S. companies lost their research coverage between January 2002 and June 2005.[44] A 2007 survey by First Call reported that 44 percent of the 1,500 NASDAQ companies had no research analyst coverage, and 14 percent were covered by only one analyst.[45]

In addition, the quality of analysts who remained in the industry was seen to suffer. The exodus of talent meant that many of the best analysts exited, and firms weren't willing to pay up to replace them with quality people, resulting in a "dumbing down" of Wall Street research. One buy-side manager cited a specific example, "Citibank just let George Shapiro go—30 years of experience, #1 aerospace and defense analyst on Wall Street. And they replaced him with a new associate. How is this guy supposed to add value?"

Consistent with concerns about declines in the quality of sell-side research at the leading banks, we find that, for the period 2002 to 2007, consensus revenue and EPS forecasts by analysts at the leading eleven banks were less accurate than those issued by analysts at other firms. The leading bank analysts' average absolute forecast errors for revenue (earnings) forecasts were 0.7 to 0.9 percent (1.0 to 1.5 percent) higher than those for other analysts. We also found that the newsworthiness of revisions of earnings estimates, measured by the stock market reaction to forecast revisions, deteriorated sharply for analysts at the eleven leading banks in 2003 and remained at the lower level through 2007. During the period we studied (2002 to 2007), the market reaction to comparable size forecast revisions were roughly 0.5 percent lower for analysts at the leading banks than for other analysts.

These findings are quite different from those reported by Cowen, Groysberg, and Healy, as will be discussed in Chapter 6, which covered the period prior to 2002 and documented that analysts at the bulge investment banks issued less optimistic and more accurate forecasts than non–bulge-bracket bank analysts.[46]

Impact on Independent Research

At the same time that the Settlement's new rules were leading large investment banks to cut back on research funding, they breathed life into the independent research market. Under the Settlement, $450 million was set aside by ten of the largest banks to pay for independent research to be distributed to clients with their own research for a period of five years. The Settlement therefore provided the seed money to support fledgling new competitors to the traditional research powerhouses.

Some of the leading sell-side analysts took advantage of the opportunities created by the new rules to leave their bulge-bracket research departments and set up their own research firms. For example, Ivy Zelman, a home building analyst, left Credit Suisse; Dana Telsey, a thirteen-year *II* ranked retail industry analyst, left Bear Stearns; Meredith Whitney, a banking analyst, left CIBC Oppenheimer; and Ed Wolfe, a transportation analyst, left Bear Stearns. One sell-side analyst described his motivations for leaving a bulge-bracket firm and starting an independent research operation:

> I want to do this because I'm not making enough, I'm not getting paid as much, I don't like working in this bureaucratic environment anymore, and I'd like to have more fun doing it . . . At the same time your entrepreneurial drive kicks in and you want to grow it [the business].

As a result of the influx of new talent and funding for independent research, many industry observers believed that the Settlement had played an important role in improving the quality of independent research. As one independent consultant explained:

> When the Settlement was first implemented, the independent research out there was crap. I reviewed 1,400 reports a quarter and sent out three

to five emails a day seven days a week, telling the independent research providers to fix their errors. The quality has been improving lately and the Settlement has played a big role in professionalizing the research industry.

In the years immediately following the global settlement, independent firms increased their market share. According to Greenwich surveys, independent firms' research share increased from 2.5 percent in 2004 to 4.0 percent in 2006.

However, funding for independent research under the Settlement ended in the summer of 2009, raising questions about its long-term viability. Industry observers anticipated that the Settlement banks would discontinue purchasing independent research for their clients beyond 2009, especially considering how little it was used.[47] The independent firms' market share appears to have stalled at 4 percent. Greenwich Associates consultant Jay Bennett opined:

> That trend appears to have run its course for now, with independents topping out at roughly 4% of overall share of the U.S. institutional research/advisory vote . . . Although the settlement changed the dynamics of the industry to a certain extent, it did not change the fact that independent research is still a very tough business. And that is in spite of the recent proliferation of commission sharing arrangements that actually makes it easier for third-party research providers to get paid.[48]

Conclusions

The Global Settlement had a significant impact on sell-side research. The changes agreed to by the largest investment banks arose from regulatory perceptions that investment banking had corroded the quality and independence of sell-side research. The new rules placed significant limits on the interactions between sell-side research and investment banking. As a result, the leading investment banks cut their research budgets by reducing head count and compensation. Many top-rated analysts joined the buy-side or hedge funds, whereas others started their own independent research boutiques to take advantage of the funds available for independent research under the Settlement. As a result of these changes, the quantity and quality of independent research increased following the Settlement.

5

Challenges to Trading Commission Model

The Global Settlement weakened the investment banking model for funding sell-side research but, as Prudential management learned when the firm exited investment banking and moved to a trading/commissions model for funding sell-side research, the trading model had its own challenges, caused by multiple developments.

Regulation Fair Disclosure (Reg FD) had a major impact; it was enacted in 2000 in response to concern that sell-side analysts' relationships with corporate managers had impaired their independence and unfairly disadvantaged investors who had no such access. In addition, the availability of new low-cost sources of company information through websites and the business media democratized information, leading to increased competition for sell-side research departments. Furthermore, the creation of efficient online trading networks reduced trading costs and commissions. Prudential managers ultimately concluded that the profitability profile of a brokerage business without investment banking was not attractive, causing them to dispose of a majority interest in their retail brokerage operations via a joint venture with Wachovia in 2003 and, eventually, to exit sell-side research entirely.

Regulatory Challenges
Analyst Relationships with Corporate Managers

Prior to the enactment of Reg FD, in the highly competitive world of sell-side research where potentially dozens of analysts may cover the same firm, access to corporate managers was a crucial way for analysts to improve the quality of their work and add value for their clients. For their part, CEOs and other top executives had considerable discretion to decide how much information to make available to each analyst. An analyst's closeness to the company's management therefore provided a special edge, leading many analysts to consider CEOs of the companies they covered as one of their major indirect reports.[1] Managers thus had leverage over the analysts covering their companies and could choose to reward those analysts who issued favorable research and to penalize those who issued negative reports.

For example, managers could reward or punish sell-side analysts by providing or restricting access to conference calls and one-on-one discussions. Management invited select analysts and institutional investors to hear discussions concerning the latest company event, such as an earnings announcement or merger, and to respond with follow-up questions. In addition, at private meetings managers could selectively provide detailed financial projections on their companies, information that some argued analysts used as the basis for their models in place of independent analysis. As analyst Michael Mayo described:

> Before getting to Wall Street, I was amazed by the way analysts could publish such precise, insightful reports on the companies they covered. I thought they must just be amazingly talented at their jobs. But that wasn't it—they were getting their information directly from the companies, often in winks and nods during private meetings with management. In some cases, analysts would show their spreadsheets to a bank's CFO [chief financial officer] and ask what he thought. The CFO would point to a certain column and say, "Hmmm, that seems a little conservative to me." The analyst would put a new number in and look expectantly at the CFO, who would smile. Message received.[2]

Concerns about sell-side analysts' independence from the corporate managers of firms they covered were not without some foundation. In

1995, Roger Lipton of Lipton Financial Services Inc., an independent research boutique, was barred from attending a Boston Chicken, Inc., investor conference after publicly criticizing the company.[3] In 1997, All-America regional bank analyst Thomas K. Brown wrote a critical report on First Union Corporation indicating that Chairman Edward E. Crutchfield Jr.'s salary had increased significantly while the stock underperformed the market. A frustrated Crutchfield flew to New York to confront Brown, who stood by his evaluation. Brown was later barred from First Union Corporation's headquarters after he and Crutchfield publicly exchanged heated words, and he was subsequently fired by DLJ.[4]

While these examples are extreme, the so-called selective disclosure practices used by some companies to share information with favored analysts had obvious rewards and provided incentives for analysts to be guarded in criticizing the companies and management teams they covered.

Regulation Fair Disclosure

In December 1999, the U.S. Securities and Exchange Commission (SEC) proposed Regulation Fair Disclosure to ban selective management disclosures to analysts and portfolio managers. The SEC argued that selective disclosure was unfair to investors who had no such access to private information. Investors with this inside information could "make a profit or avoid a loss at the expense of those kept in the dark."[5] As a result, the SEC argued, "Investors who see a security's price change dramatically and only later are given access to the information responsible for that move rightly question whether they are on a level playing field with market insiders."[6]

In addition to increasing investor confidence, the SEC contended that the new rules would limit managers' ability to reward analysts who recommended their stock through access to information and to penalize analysts who were critical of the company.

Finally, the SEC noted that technological advances facilitated broader dissemination of information than previously possible. "Whereas issuers once may have had to rely on analysts to serve as information intermediaries, issuers now can use a variety of methods to communicate directly with the market. In addition to press releases, these methods include, among others, Internet webcasting and teleconferencing. . . . Technological limitations no longer provide an excuse for abiding the threats to market integrity that selective disclosure represents."[7] Consistent with this argument, an earnings release conference call with 100 phone lines cost around $200,000, whereas a webcast with the same size audience was only $400.[8]

During the public comment period, the SEC received a record 5,000 letters on its proposal. The majority supported the recommended changes, but large institutional investors, accustomed to benefiting from selectively disclosed material information, argued that the proposed rules would lead to less disclosure. On August 10, 2000, the new regulation was approved.

Under the new regulation, which became effective on October 23, 2000, corporate management was prohibited from providing private disclosure of material information to particular analysts or investors. If management unintentionally provided such information, it was required to disclose the information publicly within twenty-four hours.

Impact of Regulation Fair Disclosure

The impact of Reg FD on sell-side research has been a popular topic for scholarly research. Some have focused on the impact of the new rules on conference calls; others have looked at its effect on the value of sell-side research.

Impact on Conference Calls

Brian Bushee, Dawn Matsumoto, and Greg Miller examine whether Reg FD stifled management conference call disclosures, as some feared.[9] To provide evidence on this question, they analyze how firms directly affected by the new rules—firms that had previously restricted access to conference calls to favored analysts and portfolio managers—responded to the change. Did they discontinue conference calls, open calls to all investors, or continue with the closed format while taking care not to disclose material new information?

One challenge for the researchers in analyzing the responses of these firms is that Reg FD coincided with a number of other important events that could potentially have also influenced managers' conference call decisions. The change came in the midst of the tech stock collapse and was followed soon after by the fall of Enron and a wave of accounting scandals. Whether these events increased or decreased the frequency of corporate conference calls is unclear, but it was certainly a time of turbulence. To control for these and any other potentially confounding events, Bushee, Matsumoto, and Miller compare the behavior of firms affected by Reg

FD to control firms that had open access conference calls prior to the regulatory change. Any factors other than Reg FD that influenced conference call decisions would presumably also influence the control firms.

The study finds that 96.4 percent of firms that restricted access to calls prior to the regulatory change continued hosting calls (making them open to all investors) afterward, compared to 98.2 percent for the control firms. Consequently, managers of the firms most affected by the new rules did not eliminate conference calls following the regulation, as some had feared.

Of course, this evidence does not directly examine whether disclosure declined following Reg FD. Managers of firms who chose to host an open conference call in response to the new regulation may have actually reduced the information they provided to the market by being more careful about what was disclosed at the new open calls. To explore this possibility, Bushee, Matsumoto, and Miller compare the newsworthiness of conference calls before and after Reg FD, measuring newsworthiness by the absolute value of stock returns on the call date. The measure therefore reflects any new information on the stock, good or bad, that reached the market on that date.

They find no discernible decline in the newsworthiness of conference calls following the regulation for either firms that restricted calls prior to Reg FD or those that had consistently hosted open calls. They conclude that managers who had restricted access to calls prior to the Reg FD did not reduce the amount of information they disclosed in calls after the new rules were in effect.

Impact on Value of Analysts' Research

A second question that has received attention from academics is how Reg FD affected the value of financial analysts' research. If the new rules were effective in reducing or even eliminating sell-side analysts' access to proprietary information, their research would become less valuable. Andreas Gintschel and Stanimir Markov examine stock volatility at the time of analyst forecast and recommendation announcements in the years before and after Reg FD.[10] Stock volatility provides a way of measuring the market reaction to analyst reports, be it good or bad news. If analysts' research became less valuable after Reg FD, the stock volatility at their earnings and recommendation changes would decline.

They find that there was a 28 percent decline in stock volatility at the announcements after the regulation. The decline was particularly pronounced for stocks with high price-to-book multiples, for analysts at highly ranked banks and brokerage firms, and for analysts who had been most optimistic prior to Reg FD. They interpret these findings as indicating that Reg FD was effective in reducing the information advantage for analysts covering difficult to value stocks, for analysts at the leading brokerage firms, and for optimistic analysts, all of whom were likely to benefit from early access to management information pre–Reg FD.

Reg FD thus does appear to have contributed to changing the competitive landscape for sell-side banks and brokerage firms. Banks whose analysts were formerly able to add value through their access to management information (perhaps as a result of their involvement in banking deals) no longer held the same advantage. A more level playing field presumably allowed talented analysts at midsized banks and research boutiques to compete more effectively.

Analyst Responses to Reg FD

Analysts have reacted to the changes in access to management by searching for private information from new sources such as customers and suppliers of firms they covered and by increasing coverage of firms where their research was more likely to add value for clients.[11] As one research department manager commented:

> It changed very much the focus of the analysts and what we highlighted, what we staffed up the analysts for, or we gave the analysts airtime for. All the directions shifted toward proprietary, anticipatory, hopefully money-making work, and away from the day-to-day maintenance, as we always called it.

In addition, loopholes in the new regulation changed but did not eliminate management interactions with analysts and leading institutional investors. Although Reg FD disallowed companies from selectively disclosing any new material information to analysts, executives at firms could go into greater detail about previously released issues.[12] Access to top management therefore continues to be important, albeit harder to get, especially as company earnings calls became more scripted with less time devoted to answering analyst questions. Michael Mayo testified before Congress two years after the enactment of Reg FD about the continued importance of corporate access and the pressure that this put on sell–side analysts:

> Objective analysts, those with negative opinions and/or critical remarks, may have trouble holding corporations accountable. The reason is that companies themselves and their managements are the best source of information, and bullish and conflicted analysts may have the best access to this information. . . . It is still hard for an analyst to be objective and critical. When an analyst says "Sell," there can be backlash from investors who own the stock, from the company being scrutinized, and even from individuals inside the analyst's firm. While much attention in Washington is being paid to the pressures related to a firm's investment banking operations, other pressures can be as great or more. The main point: Some companies may intimidate analysts into being bullish. Those who stand up may face less access to company information and perhaps backlashes, too.[13]

In the new environment, analysts found themselves brokering meetings between fund managers and company executives.[14] As one former sell–side analyst who subsequently joined a hedge fund explained:

> Sell-side analysts get company management teams to meet with them in a place like Las Vegas. Then the hedge funds will pay that analyst's bank for management access. We pay for the meetings. We pay for company access. It's all still there. It's just in different forms.

Academic research reinforces the continued importance and value of private meetings between large investors and company executives organized by sell–side analysts. David Solomon and Eugene Soltes examine all private meetings between investors and senior management at a single mid-cap NYSE firm from November 2004 to March 2010.[15] They find that, during this period, the firm's senior management had more than 900 meetings with 340 different institutional investors, many at conferences and road shows organized by sell–side analysts and their firms. A management meeting changes the probability that a hedge fund increases or decreases its position in the company by 21 percent. These trades are profitable, enabling favored hedge fund managers to increase their holdings before high-return quarters and reduce them before quarters of low returns.

Reg FD also does not appear to be have eliminated private interactions between sell–side analysts and senior company managers. Eugene

Soltes examines private meetings between sell-side analysts and senior executives at a single large cap NYSE firm from November 2010 to October 2011.[16] During this period, senior management conducted seventy-five private meetings with analysts. The meeting analysts are more likely to update their report on the company during the meeting month, participate actively in conference calls, and facilitate buy-side meetings. But they do not show any improvement in their earnings estimates.

Technology Changes and the Commission Model

The trading commission model used to support sell-side research has also been affected by significant changes in information technology, including the democratization of information and the creation of online trading platforms.

Democratization of Information

The Internet has radically increased access to information for all investors and accelerated the speed of information dissemination. It has enabled investors to learn about important company news, such as earnings releases, acquisitions, and new contracts, virtually the instant that it is announced. The rapid dissemination of information has also had an impact on the way in which stock prices move—although, historically, long-term trends were a bigger driver of stock prices, today there is more focus on a single quarter and whether a company meets or beats analysts' earnings expectations.

In recalling how quickly times have changed, one research department manager described how analysts used to learn about and inform clients about corporate earnings releases:

> We would send a messenger over and get the earnings, spend a couple days and talk to the company, write up a note, and then maybe fax it out, or mail it out. And so information traveled very slowly, and everybody relied on the sell-side to do that kind of heavy lifting.

Today, webcast video conference calls allow investors to listen to management respond to questions about the company's performance on the day of the earnings release.

In addition, free online finance services offered by Yahoo, Google, and others publish up-to-date reports on thousands of companies, including current and historical stock prices, historical financial statements, news releases, major competitors, key business information, and analyst consensus forecasts. The web and twenty-four-hour business news cable programming enable the business media and individuals to provide a constant online stream of commentary and speculation on key events affecting a given company.

Technology has also provided a low-cost way for information intermediaries (such as sell-side analysts) to reach and communicate rapidly with current and potential customers. For sell-side analysts, research reports that were once mailed are now e-mailed; daily conversations with buy-side analysts and portfolio managers have been replaced by frequent e-mails and continuous instant messaging.

As a result of these changes, the amount of information available to investors and the speed with which it is disseminated have increased dramatically, presumably creating a more efficient U.S. equity market. Access to information on the web from companies directly and from other free online sources has reduced the value of analysts as information providers. As one sell-side analyst recalled, "Before earnings releases were omnipresent and immediately accessible, the sell-side had real value in just getting that information out there." Technology has rendered this function redundant and reduced the time and opportunity to take advantage of private information. These changes have diminished sell-side analysts' information edge in the market. Buy-side clients have increasingly placed less value on sell-side analysts as key or exclusive sources of information about company events and prospects.

The democratization of information has reinforced the need for sell-side analysts to work harder, dig deeper, and look for new sources of information to generate value for clients. Technology has facilitated their search. For example, sell-side analysts have used online tools to conduct regular surveys of customers and suppliers of companies they cover. By taking advantage of these tools, analysts have been able to monitor the customer and supply channels of the companies they cover, generating potentially valuable information for clients. For example, Dana Telsey's research firm, Telsey Advisory Group (TAG), provides detailed data points on the retailers it covers, including weekly updates on inventory levels, store traffic, and markdowns. Telsey also provides clients with direct access to TAG Metrics, a database it has compiled that includes detailed historic financial, market, and operating data.

The changes have also affected institutional investors. The proliferation of information on stocks has created a challenge of increased information overload. By the beginning of 1998, investors could use the web to gain access to research from more than 115 brokerage and independent research firms getting access to over 200,000 reports on 22,000 public companies worldwide.[17]

But the declining cost of covering a stock has also made it feasible for buy-side firms to create their own research departments. Although their analysts track many more stocks than does the sell side, they serve two valuable roles. First, they help portfolio managers screen the vast quantities of information that is issued on stocks every day, reducing the cost of information overload. And, second, the best buy-side analysts provide a unique point of view on a stock that, unlike sell-side views, is private and appropriable.

Electronic Trading and Commissions

Many buy-side firms have assigned an increasing share of their trades to electronic communication networks (ECNs). Electronic trading in single-stock trades has increased from 23 percent of all trades in 2005–2006 to 35 percent in 2009 and is expected to increase to 41 percent within three years.

"Dark pools" are one popular form of electronic trading—private trading networks where buyers and sellers indicate interests and match orders without disclosing pricing or volume details. According to TABB Group, the number of dark pools operating within the United States increased from five in 2006 to forty-two one year later. They accounted for 10 percent of equity trading volume in 2007, up from 1 percent in 2003.[18] While most brokers participate in dark pools by sponsoring their own pools and gaining access to third-party pools on their clients' behalf, many buy-side clients also trade directly, lowering their costs of trade execution.

The major brokerage firms have made significant investments in electronic trading capabilities, building or buying complex algorithms that allow them to take large client buy and sell orders and divide them into smaller pieces spread across multiple trading venues to reduce pricing, lower trading costs, and reduce the risk that trade positions are detected by other market participants. Brokers with leading electronic trading platforms have seen up to 70 percent of their trades implemented electronically.

Electronic trading is frequently referred to as "penny a share" business because in some cases it has reduced the trading costs of institutional investors to less than one cent per share. Largely as a result of the growth of electronic trading platforms, average per share trade commissions in U.S. equities declined from 5 cents in 2000 to an estimated 3.2 cents in 2007.[19] According to a 2007 Greenwich Associates survey, the average commission on full-service trades was 3.8 cents versus only 1.8 cents for self-directed electronic trades.[20] Although the drop in commission rates has been accompanied by robust growth in equity trading volumes, this growth has not been sufficient to offset the rate decline. According to a Greenwich Associates study, aggregate U.S. equity commissions declined from $13.4 billion in 2002 to $10.8 billion in 2005–2006–2007.[21] They rose again to $13.45 billion in 2008–2009 but declined to $10.86 billion in 2011–2012.[22] Approximately 47 percent of commissions were generated by traditional institutional asset managers, 30 percent by hedge funds, and 23 percent by mutual funds.[23] (See Exhibit 5.1.)

As a result of the decline in industry commission revenues, fewer funds are available for funding research. Peter Forlenza, former cohead of equities

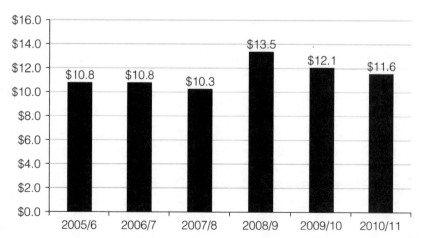

Exhibit 5.1. Investment bank and brokerage firm commission revenues for the period 2005–2011 (in billions of dollars).

SOURCE: Greenwich Associate data as reported in Josee Rose, "Brokers' Commissions Drop as Electronic Trading Grows," *Associated Press Newswires*, August 22, 2007, via Factiva, retrieved in June 2011; John D'antona Jr., "Commissions Off-Pressure Remains," *Traders Magazine*, July 1, 2010, via Factiva, retrieved in June 2011; and Greenwich Advisors, "Stock Research Gains, E-Trading Slips in Shift," *Futures*, June 21, 2011, via Factiva, retrieved in June 2011.

at Banc of America Securities, observed, "Every dollar paid into a dark pool that is not run by a sell-side entity is a dollar that is not being reinvested back into research and other products they can take advantage of."[24]

Some leading buy-side firms have responded to the decline in trade execution costs by restructuring the way they pay for research and trade execution. Instead of paying a bundled commission to cover these combined costs, the firms agreed to make cash payments for research and were charged commission rates solely to cover trade execution costs. The revised model ensured that they were able to take full financial advantage of the lower costs of trading. For example, Fidelity signed such a deal with Lehman Brothers in 2005, agreeing to pay a reported $7 million per annum for research and 2.5 cents per share for trade execution.[25] According to one sell-side research department manager, cash payments for research comprised approximately 10 percent of total departmental revenues in 2009, up from 5 percent several years earlier.

Impact on the Research Industry

The Global Settlement, Reg FD, and technology changes have changed the industry's competitive landscape over the last decade. From 1992 to 2002, the number of sell-side analysts in the United States grew by 118 percent for the industry as a whole and by 125 percent for bulge-bracket firms. However, from 2002 to 2004, the regulatory and technological shocks discussed in this book, as well as turbulent financial markets, were accompanied by a 13 percent decline in the number of sell-side analysts and an 18 percent drop for the bulge firms. (See Exhibit 5.2.)

Exhibit 5.2   Number of sell-side analysts and firms industry-wide and number of analysts at bulge-bracket firms.

	1982	1989	1992	1997	2000	2002	2004	2011
Number of sell-side firms	316	325	304	514	421	416	422	455
Number of sell-side analysts	1,915	3,021	2,937	5,834	6,498	6,421	5,595	5,872
Number of bulge firm analysts	270	359	419	607	783	941	769	883
Average number analysts per firm								
Nonbulge	5	8	8	10	14	13	12	11
Bulge	45	60	70	101	131	157	128	147

SOURCE: Nelson Information, Inc., "Nelson's Directory of Investment Research" (Port Chester, NY: Nelson, 1982–2005). Thomson One, retrieved in March 2011.

By 2011, the industry had recovered somewhat, although it employed roughly the same number of analysts as in 1997. It is interesting to note that, despite the regulatory changes that reduced opportunities to monetize research through investment banking, bulge-bracket firms employed a larger share of industry analysts in 2011 than in 2000 (15 percent versus 12 percent), suggesting that they were able to leverage costly investments in trading platforms to generate a larger share of the institutional trading business, some of which was allocated to research. However, although bulge firms employed a greater share of sell-side analysts in 2011, earlier evidence of a relative decline in the accuracy of their analysts' earnings estimates (after 2004) raises questions about the quality of these firms' analysts.

In 2011, there was also a modest increase in the number of nonbulge sell-side firms. By lowering the cost and increasing the speed of accessing comprehensive information on firms, information technology facilitated the production of research by boutique firms. For example, veteran equity analyst Ivy Zelman formed Zelman and Associates in 2007. The firm created a monthly survey of building and housing products that had become a leading indicator of the housing market. David Zelman, the firm's president, explained how the firm used technology to construct its main research product:

> Ivy [Zelman] has built a massive barter network. We give our research to hundreds of executives around the country, it's encrypted. In order to barter with us, you have to be a meaningful company at some part of the housing food chain. In exchange for the research, you have to, once a month, fill out online surveys and/or talk to our analysts gathering information real-time about their businesses . . . We are asking them about the trends in their business and about what they are seeing. . . . So we are a giant sieve and repository of real-time information; none of this would be happening if it wasn't for Ivy and her team's proven ability to analyze and synthesize a massive amount of data into thoughtful, proprietary, and action oriented investment conclusions that have proven to be accurate time and time again. As you can imagine, getting all these real world companies to share information with us is no easy feat.

Finally, the technology changes described in this chapter made it cost effective for buy-side firms to support their own research departments.

Exhibit 5.3 Number of analysts employed by the buy-side industry and by the twenty largest money management firms by AUM.

	2002	2003	2004	2005	2008
All firms					
Number of firms	1,011	1,012	1,027	985	843
Number of funds	8,393	8,533	8,418	8,471	8,797
Number of professionals	19,680	19,231	17,368	15,993	25,158
Number of portfolio managers and analysts	7,793	7,559	7,467	7,323	7,470
Funds per firm	8.3	8.4	8.2	8.6	10.4
Professionals per firm	19.5	19.0	16.9	16.2	29.8
Portfolio managers and analysts per firm	7.7	7.5	7.3	7.4	8.9
Top twenty firms					
Number of funds	911	921	1,081	1,114	1,168
Number of professionals	3,362	3,359	2,985	2,671	3,612
Number of portfolio managers and analysts	1,186	1,076	952	882	1,085
Funds per firm	45.6	46.1	54.1	55.7	58.4
Professionals per firm	168.1	168.0	149.3	133.6	180.6
Portfolio managers and analysts per firm	59.3	53.8	47.6	44.1	54.3

SOURCE: Nelson Information, Inc., "Nelson's Directory of Investment Managers" (Port Chester, NY: Nelson, 2002–2009).

From 2002 through 2008, the number of analysts and portfolio managers employed on the buy-side averaged around 7,500 for the full industry and 1,000 for the twenty largest firms (see Exhibit 5.3).

Conclusions

Regulation Fair Disclosure and changes in information technology, notably the democratization of information and the availability of new electronic trading platforms, have added pressure on the already vulnerable trading commission model of funding sell side. These changes, along with the Global Settlement, which weakened the investment banking funding model, have transformed the industry. The competitive advantages of analysts at the leading investment banks have diminished, leading to a decline in hiring. This has been somewhat offset by modest increases in analyst employment at midmarket banks and brokerage firms and at research boutiques. But the most significant change has been at buy-side firms, many of which have created their own research departments.

6

The Performance of Sell-Side Analysts Revisited

The evolution of research at Prudential from brokerage business to investment bank, and then back to brokerage business, raises important questions about sell-side analysts' incentives and performance. Prudential's management, as well as regulators in the early 2000s, concluded that the ties between sell-side analysts and investment banking had corroded the quality of equity research.

Evidence from the Spitzer report indicates that a few analysts at leading banks had their opinions swayed by investment banking business. But it is unclear whether the problem was widespread. The academic studies find that analysts covering banking clients were more optimistic about the firms' long-term prospects than were other analysts. But the cause and effect here is unclear. Were the analysts influenced to provide inflated assessments of the clients' prospects, as some suggest? Or did issuers simply seek out firms whose analysts and bankers were the most bullish on their prospects? Finally, there has been little evidence on how brokerage business affects sell-side analysts' research.

We revisit the question of how conflicts affect sell-side research by comparing the performance of sell-side analysts at investment banks relative to analysts at brokerage firms that do not offer banking services and to buy-side analysts who do not face conflicts from investment banking or brokerage businesses. Our findings challenge the popular view.

Contrary to concerns that analysts at investment banks produce more optimistic research, we find that prior to the Global Settlement they actually produced less biased and higher-quality research than their peers at brokerage firms. Indeed, prior to 2003, analysts at the most prestigious bulge-bracket banks were the least biased and had the highest-quality research, whereas analysts at brokerage firms with retail clients had the greatest bias, indicating that firm reputation and the retail brokerage business had powerful influences on sell-side research.

Our research on the relative performance of sell-side analysts and analysts at a top-ten buy-side firm from 1997 to 2004 shows that the sell-side analysts issued less optimistic and more accurate earnings estimates than their buy-side peers. In terms of stock recommendations, the sell-side issued more strong buys/buys and fewer sells/underperforms for a more diverse set of firms. But the performance of the sell-side analysts' buy recommendations was comparable to or better than that of their buy-side peers.

Our findings therefore indicate that, despite investment bank and brokerage conflicts, sell-side research has important strengths. The sell-side industry is highly competitive, and the performance of sell-side analysts is transparent given feedback from clients. Both these characteristics lead to speedier exits of poorly performing sell-side analysts than observed at the buy-side firm. Consequently, many of the concerns about the impact of investment banking on the quality of sell-side research may have been overstated. Some well-known sell-side analysts at investment banks certainly acted improperly. But, overall, sell-side analysts, particularly those at leading investment banks, provided clients with relatively high-quality research.

Research Funding and Analyst Performance

Concerns about analyst conflicts of interest have arisen primarily from the investment banking research funding model. However, the use of trading commissions to support research can also generate conflicts of interest. By issuing research reports with new investment ideas for their clients, sell-side analysts may be able to encourage greater portfolio churn, generating incremental commissions for the bank.

Trading incentives have historically encouraged analysts to issue investment recommendations tilted toward buys rather than sells. Until the recent growth in hedge fund trading, most institutional trading was by firms that were prohibited from shorting stocks. They typically demanded analysts to provide them with new purchase ideas and reacted negatively to sell recommendations for stocks they owned, which reduced the value of their investments and made exiting more difficult.[1] Positive reports have also been more effective in generating retail trading volume; *any* retail investor can act on a buy recommendation at relatively low cost by buying the stock, whereas negative reports can be acted on only by investors who already own the stock or who are willing to incur the additional costs of short-selling.[2]

Incentives to provide overly optimistic research are tempered for institutional clients who make no contractual commitment to pay for research prior to receiving it. They compensate the bank for research after the fact, when they have had sufficient time to fully analyze and judge its quality. Because they have access to research from many of the large banks and have their own in-house research departments, institutional investors are likely to be in a good position to evaluate research quality across banks. This leaves the bank to bear the risk that clients decide its analysts' research is worthless. Banks manage this risk by tying analysts' remuneration to feedback from institutions on the value of research on companies they follow, creating an incentive for analysts to provide high-quality research to institutional clients.[3] Consistent with this, Ljungqvist and his coauthors find that analysts' recommendations are less optimistic for stocks with heavy institutional ownership.[4]

In theory, reputation also has the potential to temper incentives for analysts to provide highly optimistic research to retail investors. Analysts who produce optimistic research may encourage retail investors to trade in the short term. Yet, in a well-functioning market, this type of investment advice is likely to be unsustainable. Investors who base their trading decisions on biased research will earn disappointing returns. Over time, they will learn to discount research from biased analysts and to seek other investment advice. Firms and analysts that produce less biased research are therefore likely to develop a reputation for research quality and to attract investors.

However, in practice, several factors are likely to reduce the alignment between the incentives of analysts and retail investors. First, retail investors typically have relationships with only one investment advisor and are less informed than institutional investors, making it difficult for them to evaluate research quality differences across firms.[5] In addition, it can be difficult for retail investors to evaluate research quality given the volatility of the market.

To evaluate how the investment banking and trading funding models affected analyst research prior to the Global Settlement, we examine differences in the optimism of analyst forecasts and recommendations at three types of firms: full-service investment banks, nonunderwriter (syndicate) banks, and brokerage firms.[6] Full-service banks provide both underwriting and brokerage services and use revenues from both to fund research.[7] Given the importance of the banking revenues, analysts at these firms had the strongest banking incentives to issue optimistic research. Nonunderwriter (syndicate) banks distributed new issues to their clients and provided brokerage services but did not underwrite new offers. These banks funded research from both distribution fees and brokerage revenues. However, investment banking incentives for these firms were considerably weaker than for full-service banks because banking fees from distribution were typically only one-sixth those from underwriting.[8] Finally, brokerage firms did not undertake investment banking activities (either underwriting or distribution); their primary source of income was commissions from client trade execution and was thus affected solely by trading conflicts of interest.

Differences in Research Optimism by Type of Firm

We assessed the optimism of analysts working at the three types of firms by examining whether their short-term and long-term earnings forecasts, target stock prices, and stock recommendations were greater than those of other analysts covering the same stocks. For each analyst earnings or price forecast, we computed the difference between individual analysts' estimates and the consensus of all analysts who covered the same stock and issued earnings and price forecasts at roughly the same date. To control for differences in uncertainty across firms, we divided these differences by the standard deviation of analyst forecasts for the firm.

Our calculations show that mean standardized forecasts for analysts at full-service banks are no different from consensus forecasts across three forecast horizons for the period January 1996 to December 2002 (see Exhibit 6.1). These results are not too surprising because analysts at full-service banks comprised roughly 85 percent of the analysts we studied prior to the Global Settlement and therefore typically represented the consensus. But analysts at brokerage and syndicate firms—firms that relied more on commission revenues to fund research—showed positive forecast optimism for one- and two-quarter-ahead earnings and for target

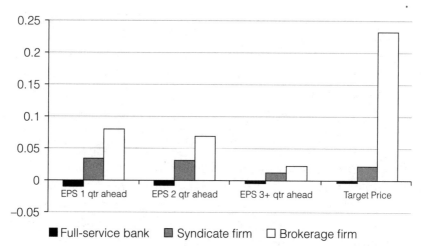

Exhibit 6.1. Relative forecast optimism of sell-side analysts forecasts of earnings per share and stock price by firm type from January 1996 to December 2002.

NOTE: Relative forecast optimism is the difference between an analyst's forecast and the consensus forecast for all analysts forecasting for the same company, quarter, and forecast horizon, divided by the standard deviation of all forecasts for the company, quarter, and horizon.

SOURCE: Amanda Paige Cowen, Boris Groysberg, and Paul Healy. "Which Types of Analyst Firms Are More Optimistic?" *Journal of Accounting & Economics* 41, nos. 1–2 (April 2006): 119–146.

prices, indicating that they were optimistic relative to their bank peers. On average, brokerage analysts' earnings forecasts exceeded those for full-service bank analysts by 4.4 percent and 3.7 percent for the one- and two-quarter horizons. For the target prices, brokerage analysts' estimates were 3.4 percent higher than those issued by their peers at full-service banks. Forecast optimism for syndicate firm analysts fell between that for full-service banks and brokerage firms.

For stock recommendations, we adopt a similar approach, computing the value of an analyst's recommendation after controlling for the type of ratings issued by other analysts covering the stock. There is little difference in recommendation optimism across analysts at full-service banks, syndicates, and brokerage firms, which implies that conflicts of interest arising from investment banking do not dominate those faced by pure brokerage firms.

In additional work, we examine a number of questions about our findings. First, the main results are for the universe of stocks covered by analysts, whereas the underwriting incentive effects are likely to be most pronounced for stocks that made new issues. Analysts at underwriter firms had stronger incentives to make optimistic forecasts about these firms to win their banking business and were less likely to be optimistic for firms that did not raise new equity capital. However, even when we restrict our analysis to firms that made IPOs and secondary offerings during the sample period, we continue to find that non–full-service bank analysts, particularly those at brokerage firms, were more optimistic than analysts at full-service banks.

Second, forecast optimism, the primary measure used in our research, is an incomplete measure of analyst forecast performance. Analysts who issue optimistic forecasts could actually turn out to be more accurate than their peers if their analysis is sound. However, this does not appear to be the case here. Tests of forecast accuracy yield findings similar to those for forecast optimism—forecasts issued by analysts at full-service banks were more accurate (as well as less optimistic) than analysts at other types of firms.

Finally, our sample period includes both the stock market boom, when underwriter research was presumed to be most biased, and the subsequent crash period, when underwriting and incentives for research bias plummeted. Yet the relative optimism of analysts at non–full-service banks and particularly brokerage firms holds for both the periods before and after April 2000 (when the NASDAQ was at its peak).

Explaining Brokerage Firm Analyst Optimism

One potential explanation for the less optimistic forecasts of underwriters is that they tend to have higher status in the industry and rely at least partially on their reputations to attract clients, rather than on optimistic analyst research. Consistent with this explanation, prior to the Global Settlement, earnings forecasts and recommendations by analysts at high-status bulge-bracket banks (Credit Suisse First Boston, Goldman Sachs, Merrill Lynch, Morgan Stanley Dean Witter, Salomon Smith Barney, and Lehman Bros.) were less optimistic than those made by analysts at non–bulge-bracket banks. Non–bulge-bracket full-service bank analysts also made less optimistic forecasts of earnings and target prices than brokerage firm analysts did. Firm status therefore appears to play a powerful role in tempering the effect of conflicts of interest.

The relative optimism of brokerage firms could also reflect brokerage incentives to provide low-quality research to retail investors, either because it is more costly for retail investors to infer quality or because recent industry changes make it difficult to charge retail investors for research. We find some evidence to support this view. Analysts at firms with both retail and institutional brokerage businesses made more optimistic earnings forecasts and stock recommendations than analysts at purely institutional trading firms.

Overall our findings indicate that prior to the Global Settlement brokerage incentives to bias research were at least as important as those of investment banking. Of course, this is not to suggest that investment banking does not have any effect on sell-side analysts' behavior. Both brokerage and banking businesses create conflicts of interest for sell-side analysts, as has been recognized by buy-side clients for many years. However, our findings show that, even during the period when concern about investment banking conflicts was at its peak, brokerage incentives had a comparable effect on analysts' stock recommendations and a greater effect on their earnings and price forecasts. Firm reputation and retail brokerage played some role in explaining these findings.

Sell-Side versus Buy-Side Research

At a fundamental level, buy- and sell-side research analysts perform similar functions. Both study companies to make recommendations about whether to buy, sell, or hold specific securities. The tasks they perform to generate their stock picks are similar—evaluating firms' business models, forecasting short-term earnings, and building financial models of stock prices. Both write reports to communicate their analysis and recommendations, including earnings forecasts, stock price projections, the recommendation, and a justification for the recommendation, as well as an overview of the firm's business.

But, as our study of a top-ten buy-side firm and interviews with buy- and sell-side firms indicates, there are fundamental differences between buy- and sell-side research and methods of compensation for both types of analysts. These differences include the scale and scope of coverage, the types of companies recommended, the sources of information used for research, the method of disseminating information, and the target audiences.

Scale and Scope of Coverage

Research departments at money management firms are typically considerably smaller than those at sell-side firms. For example, from 1997 to 2004, the research department at a top ten buy-side firm we studied employed twenty to thirty analysts compared to 186 senior analysts employed by the average bulge investment bank.

The fact that research departments at buy-side firms are smaller implies that buy-side analysts cover more companies and provide less in-depth analysis on any given stock. Analysts at buy-side firms are often responsible for covering an entire sector, such as technology. Of the fifty to 100 stocks they follow in the sector, buy-side analysts write reports on roughly fifteen stocks at any given time. In contrast, a sell-side analyst usually covers only one segment of an industry, such as semiconductors or biotech. While they also write reports on only ten to fifteen stocks at a given time, this number usually represents a much larger fraction of the total stocks they follow.

Perhaps as a result of these differences in scope, reports by analysts at the sample buy-side firm are shorter in length, typically only two pages, compared to those provided by the leading sell-side analysts, who also include detailed industry analysis and bottom-up firm-level analysis.

Types of Companies Covered

Given the scope of their coverage and the demands of portfolio managers to invest in liquid stocks to enable their relatively large positions to be unloaded with minimal impact on price, buy-side analysts are likely to cover less volatile and more liquid stocks than their sell-side peers. Stocks recommended as strong buy/buy by analysts at the buy-side firm we studied during the period 1997 to 2004 had an average daily standard deviation of abnormal returns of 0.42 percent and market capitalization of $9.1 billion, versus 0.95 percent and $1.3 billion for the average sell-side firm analyst.

Information Sources

Sell-side analysts spend as much as 30 percent of their time communicating and marketing their ideas to other analysts interested in the same sector, to sales force representatives and traders at their firm, and to clients. Through these interactions, sell-side analysts subject their ideas to broad scrutiny, which can potentially generate valuable new information and feedback. For example, traders and the sales force provide analysts with data on observed changes in trading volumes and planned purchases or sales by influential clients. Institutional investors push analysts on their analysis and conclusions. As one sell-side analyst commented, "One of the biggest roles of an analyst is to be essentially a bumblebee . . . you'll talk to one client, they will give you an idea, and then you will pollinate all other clients with that idea. You act as a central node for dispersing ideas." Sell-side analysts whom we interviewed commented that their research improves significantly through these interactions. In contrast, buy–side analysts do not have the opportunity for such diverse feedback and new insights. They have fewer colleagues with whom to debate their ideas and instead pitch their recommendations only to their own portfolio managers and their staff.

In addition, sell–side analysts frequently meet with senior managers of the firms that they cover. Analysts on both the sell side and buy side stress the importance of such meetings. As one portfolio manager opined, "You're meeting with the CEO and the CFO . . . you can make judgments about people, trying to understand their strategy, trying to understand what their long–term financial targets are for things like margins and returns on capital, returns on equity, and financial structures, and things like that." Concern that this access could potentially provide sell–side analysts with an unfair advantage over other investors led the SEC to approve Regulation Fair Disclosure in August 2000.

Private versus Public Report Dissemination

There are several implications of the fact that sell–side research is widely disseminated to institutional and retail clients, whereas buy–side research is private and only available to the buy–side firm's portfolio managers. First, it enables the investment benefits from superior research to be more effectively internalized on the buy side than on the sell side, making buy–side research easier to fund. Portfolio managers can capitalize on a buy–side analyst's new ideas by buying recommended stocks and selling those predicted to underperform ahead of other investors. If the analyst's ideas have merit, recommended stocks will appreciate in value, and those predicted to underperform will decline. In contrast, in an efficient capital market, any insights from public sell–side reports will be rapidly reflected in prices, making it difficult for clients to benefit from acting on recommendations. As a result, sell–side recommendations are likely to be of limited investment value to investors, making it more challenging to fund sell–side research.

A second implication of the private dissemination of buy–side research is that buy–side analysts are less likely to face pressure to write positive reports from managers of companies they cover. Prior to Regulation Fair Disclosure, the SEC alleged that sell–side analysts' dependence on access to managers for information could make them reluctant to issue negative reports on stocks. In contrast, buy–side analysts relied less on manager information, and their conclusions were not visible to managers of firms they covered.

Implications of Different Target Audiences

Buy- and sell-side analysts also differ in terms of their target audience. Buy-side analysts make recommendations to their firm's portfolio managers, who have ultimate authority for deciding whether to buy or sell stocks. Buy-side analysts add value for portfolio managers in two ways. First, they filter sell-side research and company news, distilling the large amount of sell-side analysis and company news reported into a short monthly report that portfolio managers and their staff can use more easily. Acting in this capacity, buy-side analysts can add value to portfolio managers by directing them to particular sell-side reports that they believe are interesting or newsworthy.

A second role for buy-side analysts is to provide the firm's portfolio managers with additional perspectives on companies. Buy-side analysts are expected to do more than simply reiterate sell-side analysts' opinions—instead they are expected to reach their own independent conclusions. If these conclusions differ materially from those of the sell-side, buy-side analysts have an opportunity to add value to their portfolio managers. In describing this role, one analyst explained:

> My job is to analyze the fundamentals of companies, to meet with the management teams, to read all of the filings, to read all of the transcripts from all of the quarterly calls, to understand their business to the extent that I can. I forecast what I think the income statement, balance sheet, and cash flows will be for the next ten years and create a model, determine the fair value [of these companies], and figure out if the stock is trading above or below that. And once I figure all that out, . . . I put out notes, an initiation note when I pick up the company and then periodic notes when I change my ratings, and I go around and talk to the portfolio managers about what I think, whether they should buy it, whether they should sell it, add to it, or trim it.

In contrast, sell-side research is distributed to buy-side analysts and portfolio managers at a wide range of firms, as well as to retail investors. Sell-side analysts' roles and value differ widely by type of client. For institutional investors, their role is to provide information on an industry and a firm's positioning within its industry, to update clients on important stock news, to facilitate meetings with management, and to provide new investment ideas. Sell-side analysts also function as an information conduit for institutional investors, a source of market intelligence. As one sell-side research department manager argued:

> The buy-side is dependent on the sell-side as an information conduit. And what I mean by that is you can't have an anti-consensus opinion that turns out to be right unless you know what the other buy-side players in that specific stock and market are thinking. [The buy-side analysts] need the sell-side because they're talking to all of the players . . . on a daily basis, or on a weekly basis, to 50 people that are actively in that name. And if you have a top analyst they are a major information conduit.

The differing target audiences of buy- and sell-side analysts create fundamental differences in incentives. Sell-side analysts create value for their firms by providing clients with research and services that generate additional trading volume in stocks covered or increased demand for a new issue that their firms underwrite or distribute, generating the conflicts of interest discussed previously. In addition, public rankings by *Institutional Investor* and the public dissemination of their research provide sell-side analysts with an incentive to follow the crowd, consistent with theories of herd behavior.

In contrast, buy-side analysts have very different incentives. They are encouraged to present portfolio managers with a fresh perspective on stocks that are currently owned and stocks that are not owned but that are attractive buys. As a result, they are likely to be more willing to make recommendations and forecasts that differ from the Street's consensus and to issue both sell and buy recommendations.

Compensation

Management at the top-ten investment firm we studied reported that in 2004 buy-side analysts' salaries averaged $300,000, and bonuses were effectively capped at roughly twice an analyst's salary. The top analysts at the firm made roughly $1 million in salary and bonus. Bonus awards were based on two factors—the performance of the analyst's buy recommendations (measured by holding returns adjusted for returns on the Standard & Poor's [S&P] 500 Index) and the impact of research on portfolio managers (measured by portfolio managers' ratings of whether the analyst provided good stock ideas, communicated those ideas effectively, made good judgment calls, and so on).

Analyst promotions at the same firm were primarily to higher levels within the research department, with accompanying increases in compensation. The firm intended successful analysts to have lengthy careers as analysts with opportunities for growth and development within the department. In contrast, some other firms in the industry have viewed analysts as "portfolio managers in training." The analyst function is then considered to be an entry position, with analysts rotated among industries to receive broad industry exposure. The most successful analysts are eventually promoted to portfolio manager, which is typically a more highly remunerated position.[9]

In contrast, compensation for sell-side analysts has historically been tied to metrics such as commissions and soft dollar revenues in the stocks they cover, their *Institutional Investor* ranking, feedback provided by institutional buy-side clients, and, prior to the Global Settlement, their ability to create demand for a new issue that their firm is underwriting or distributing.

These forms of compensation generally reinforce the differing roles and incentives of buy- and sell-side analysts. Buy-side analysts are rewarded for providing portfolio managers with new ideas that might differ from the Street consensus and that turn out to be profitable investments. Sell-side analysts are rewarded for creating new business for their firm, either by generating trading volume in the stocks they cover or, before the Global Settlement, by generating demand for new issues that their company underwrites or distributes.

Performance of Buy- and Sell-Side Analysts' Earnings Estimates

To examine how the above differences in buy- and sell-side jobs affect their relative performance, we use data from a top-ten–rated money management firm for which fundamental research is an essential part of its stock selection process. For analysts at the buy-side firm we compare the optimism of their earnings estimates and stock recommendations, the accuracy of their earnings estimates, and the performance of their stock recommendations, all relative to those of analysts at sell-side firms. The sample period is from July 1997 to December 2004.

Relative Earnings Forecast Optimism

Our measure of relative forecast optimism is similar to that described earlier in this chapter. Buy-side analysts were judged to be optimistic if they issued more positive earnings forecasts for a firm than other analysts covering the same stock. For each buy- and sell–side analyst earnings forecast, we compute the difference between the analyst's estimate and the consensus for all sell–side analysts who covered the same stock and issued earnings forecasts at roughly the same date. To control for differences in uncertainty across firms, we divide these differences by the standard deviation of analyst forecasts for the firm.

The distributions of relative optimism for all buy- and sell–side analysts' earnings forecasts (without controlling for horizon) are shown in Exhibit 6.2. The difference between the two distributions is striking. Sell–side analysts' earnings forecasts were tightly clustered around the consensus, whereas buy-side analysts had many more forecasts that were much greater than the consensus, implying that buy-side analysts were much more likely to issue optimistic forecasts than their sell–side peers.

After controlling for analyst experience and other factors that have been shown to influence analyst optimism, we find that, for a typical firm with earnings per share of $2, the average difference between buy- and sell–side estimates was $0.15 for forecasts issued three months or less ahead of year end, $0.17 for forecasts made ten to twelve months ahead, and $0.33 per share for forecast made eighteen or more months ahead.

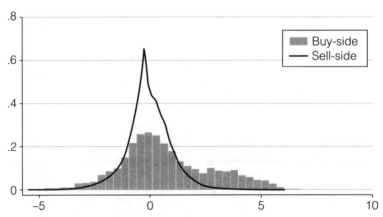

Exhibit 6.2. Distribution of relative earnings forecast optimism for analysts at a top-ten buy-side firm and sell-side analysts from July 1997 to December 2004.

NOTE: Relative earnings forecast optimism is the difference between an analyst's forecast and the average forecast for all analysts forecasting for the same company, quarter, and forecast horizon, divided by the standard deviation of forecasts for the company, quarter, and horizon.

SOURCE: Boris Groysberg, Paul M. Healy, and Craig James Chapman. "Buy-Side vs. Sell-Side Analysts' Earnings Forecasts." *Financial Analysts Journal* 64, no. 4 (July–August 2008), p. 29.

Relative Earnings Forecast Accuracy

As noted earlier in this chapter, analysts who issue optimistic forecasts could actually turn out to be more accurate than their peers if their analysis is sound. We therefore examine relative forecast accuracy for buy- and sell-side analysts. The relative accuracy of a buy- or sell-side analyst's earnings estimate is the absolute value of the forecast error (the difference between the forecast and actual earnings) less the mean absolute error for all sell-side forecasts issued for the same stock, forecast horizon, and issue date. To control for differences in uncertainty across firms, we deflate these differences by the standard deviation of absolute forecast errors for all sell-side estimates issued at the same date for the same company and horizon. Positive standardized differences indicate that the analyst's absolute forecast error is greater (or less accurate) than that for the consensus. Negative values imply the absolute error for an analyst's forecast is less than (or more accurate) than the consensus forecast.

The distributions of relative accuracy for all buy- and sell-side analysts' earnings forecasts covering all forecast horizons are shown in Exhibit 6.3. The difference between the two distributions is very similar to that shown for relative forecast optimism. Sell-side analysts' absolute forecast errors

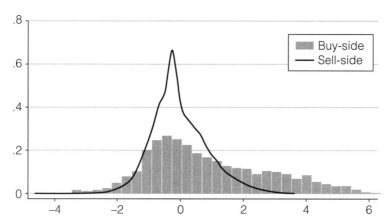

Exhibit 6.3. Distribution of relative earnings forecast accuracy for analysts at a top-ten buy-side firm and sell-side analysts for the period July 1997 to December 2004.

NOTE: Relative earnings forecast accuracy is the difference between the absolute value of an analyst's forecast error and the average absolute forecast error for all analysts forecasting for the same company, quarter, and forecast horizon, divided by the standard deviation of absolute forecast errors for the company, quarter, and horizon.

SOURCE: Boris Groysberg, Paul M. Healy, and Craig James Chapman. "Buy-Side vs. Sell-Side Analysts' Earnings Forecasts." *Financial Analysts Journal* 64, no. 4 (July–August 2008), p. 31.

are tightly clustered around the absolute consensus error. In contrast, buy-side analysts had many absolute errors that exceeded that of the consensus, implying that buy-side analysts are much more likely to issue inaccurate forecasts than their sell-side peers.

After controlling for analyst experience and other factors that have been shown to influence analyst optimism, we find that, for a typical firm with earnings per share of $2, the mean difference between buy- and sell-side forecast accuracy is $0.21 for forecasts issued three months or less ahead of year end, $0.18 for forecasts made ten to twelve months ahead, and $0.30 per share for those made eighteen or more months ahead.

Why Are Sell-side Analysts' Earnings Estimates Less Biased and More Accurate?

We examine several potential explanations for the more optimistic and less accurate earnings forecasts of the buy-side firm analysts.

Differences in Analyst Retention.   One explanation is that the buy-side firm retained fewer high-quality analysts or more low-quality analysts than sell-side firms. Consistent with this explanation, we find that the buy-side firm was more likely than sell-side firms to retain analysts who made inaccurate earnings estimates. Relative to their average retention rates, the buy-side firm was 2 percent *more* likely to retain analysts whose forecast accuracy ranked in the lowest 25 percent in a given year, whereas sell-side firms were 6 percent *less* likely to retain their weakest forecasters. This suggests that sell-side firms were more competitive than the buy-side firm, and replaced poor-performing analysts more promptly, consistent with their performance differences.

Differences in Buy and Sell-Side Analyst Benchmarks.   A second explanation is that buy- and sell-side analysts have different incentives. Throughout our sample period, the money management firm we studied made no attempt to benchmark buy-side analysts' performance against sell-side peers.[10] In contrast, as discussed in Chapter 3, investment banks and brokerage firms regularly compare the ratings of sell-side analysts provided by *Institutional Investor* magazine, Greenwich Associates, and by client votes.

Sell-Side Information Advantage.   We also examine whether the sell-side performance arose from an information advantage over the buy-side firm analysts. One form of information advantage could arise from sell-side analysts having superior access to information from company managers, at least prior to the adoption of Reg FD in 2000. We find that beginning in 1999 there was an increase in optimism and a decline in accuracy of forecasts issued by sell-side analysts but no such changes for analysts at the buy-side firm. This pattern continued through 2003, when buy-side analyst forecast optimism and accuracy was similar to that of sell-side peers. However, in 2004 the buy-side optimism and inaccuracy reappeared. These findings provide some evidence that sell-side analysts had an information advantage over analysts at the buy-side firm prior to Reg FD, potentially explaining our findings. However, given all of the other market changes that occurred during this period and given the reversal of the sell-side out-performance in 2004, we are cautious about reaching definite conclusions.

Differences in Analyst Quality.   To examine whether the strong performance of sell-side research is due to their hiring higher-quality analysts, we trace the performance of twenty-seven buy-side analysts who were hired from the sell side. Exhibits 6.4 and 6.5 show the distribution of relative earnings optimism and absolute forecast errors for these analysts before and after they moved to the buy side. Prior to the switch, there was little difference in optimism or absolute forecast errors between the sell-side analysts who were hired by the buy-side firm and those who continued working on the sell-side. However, after they moved to the buy-side firm, these analysts showed a higher proportion of optimistic forecasts and relatively large absolute forecast errors. This pattern appeared for stocks that the analyst continued covering at the buy-side firm and for stocks that were newly covered following the hiring change. Given these findings, it does not appear that the differential performance of sell-side analysts is due to the buy-side firm hiring lower-quality analysts than the sell-side.

Quality of the Buy-Side Firm.   Another plausible explanation for our findings is that the buy-side firm is simply a poor performer, perhaps because of its poor research performance. However, in *Reuters* and *Institutional Investor* ratings of top U.S. fund management groups from 1997 to 2003, the firm was consistently ranked among the top-ten firms. Morningstar ratings of the performance of the firm's funds relative to relevant competitor funds placed them in the top categories for one-, three-, and five-year horizons for several categories and multiple years. This suggests that, if anything, the sample firm we examined is a superior performer.

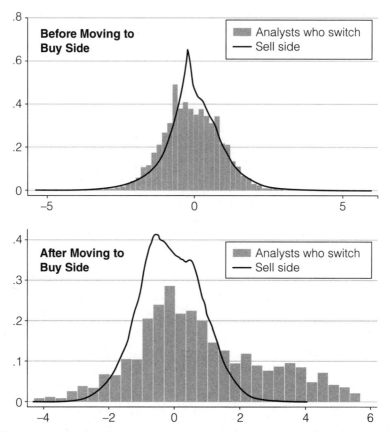

Exhibit 6.4. Distribution of relative earnings forecast optimism for buy-side analysts hired from the sell-side (before and after hiring) during the period January 1984 to December 2004.

NOTE: Relative earnings forecast optimism is the difference between an analyst's forecast and the average forecast for all analysts forecasting for the same company, quarter, and forecast horizon, divided by the standard deviation of forecasts for the company, quarter, and horizon.

SOURCE: Boris Groysberg, Paul M. Healy, and Craig James Chapman. "Buy-Side vs. Sell-Side Analysts' Earnings Forecasts." *Financial Analysts Journal* 64, no. 4 (July–August 2008), p. 35.

Differences in Scope of Analyst Coverage.   To examine how our findings are affected by differences in the scope of analyst coverage, we compared the forecast performance of the buy-side analysts to that of analysts at sell-side firms with comparable size and coverage scope. The findings were very similar to those reported in the preceding pages, indicating that differences in coverage scope probably do not explain the earnings forecast optimism and inaccuracy of the buy-side analysts.

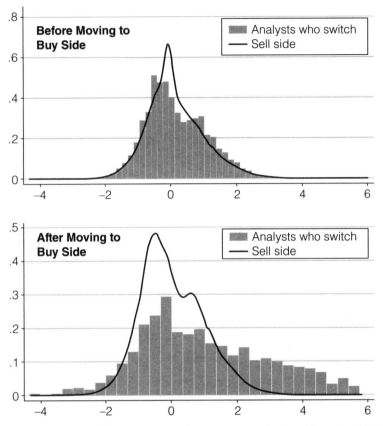

Exhibit 6.5. Distribution of relative earnings forecast accuracy for buy-side analysts hired from the sell side (before and after hiring) during the period from January 1984 to December 2004.

NOTE: Relative earnings forecast accuracy is the difference between the absolute value of an analyst's forecast error and the average absolute forecast error for all analysts forecasting for the same company, quarter, and forecast horizon, divided by the standard deviation of absolute forecast errors for the company, quarter, and horizon.

SOURCE: Boris Groysberg, Paul M. Healy, and Craig James Chapman. "Buy-Side vs. Sell-Side Analysts' Earnings Forecasts." *Financial Analysts Journal* 64, no. 4 (July–August 2008), p. 36.

Performance of Buy- and Sell-Side Analysts' Stock Recommendations
Recommendation Optimism

To examine differences in recommendation optimism for buy- and sell-side analysts, we compute the frequencies of strong buy/buy, hold, and underperform/sell ratings. Strong buys and buys are aggregated into a single category because the buy-side firm studied treated the two as synonymous for measuring analyst performance—the firm based bonus awards, in part, on returns from investing in their analysts' strong buy and buy recommendations. To be consistent with the aggregation of strong buys and buys and to overcome the small number of sell-side underperform and sell recommendations, we also combine the underperform and sell recommendations.

The frequencies of stock recommendation across the three categories for the buy- and sell-side analysts are presented in Exhibit 6.6. Buy-side analysts issued proportionately fewer strong buy/buy recommendations and more hold and underperform/sell recommendations than their peers on the sell side. Forty-four percent of the recommendations issued by the buy-side firm analysts were strong buy or buy, compared to 56 percent for sell-side analysts. In contrast, 14 percent of buy-side analyst recommendations were underperform/sell, versus 7 percent for sell-side analysts.

Recommendation Performance

To compare the recommendation performance of buy- and sell-side analysts, we measure the returns to investing in buy (strong buy/buy) recommendations for the buy-side firm and for eighty-five sell-side firms

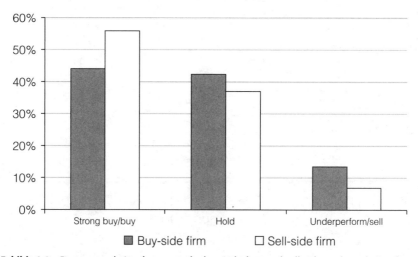

Exhibit 6.6. Recommendation frequency for buy-side firm and sell-side analysts during the period July 1997 to December 2004.

SOURCE: Boris Groysberg, Paul Healy, George Serafeim, and Devin Shanthikumar, "The Stock Selection and Performance of Buy-Side Analysts," *Management Science* (forthcoming).

that issued recommendations consistently throughout the same period.[11] We compute returns using two approaches: market–adjusted returns controlled for marketwide price fluctuations and abnormal returns controlled for risk, size, growth, and momentum factors that prior research has shown are related to stock performance.[12] We compute market–adjusted or abnormal returns for each firm by buying and holding stocks its analysts rated as buys from the day after the first buy rating until the day after there was a downgrade to hold or lower (if they continued to be covered) or for 250 days (if they ceased to be covered).[13]

Exhibit 6.7 shows market–adjusted and abnormal returns to investing in buy recommendations for the buy-side firm and the eighty-five sell-side firms. Analysts at the buy-side firm generated an annualized market-adjusted return of 2.3 percent compared to 8.2 percent per year for sell-side analysts. These findings are not attributable to a few high-performing sell-side firms. The median sell-side market-adjusted return was 7.4 percent, more than three times the median buy-side firm return. The buy-side firm's performance was ranked at the twelfth percentile relative to sell-side peers.

Exhibit 6.7 Mean annualized market-adjusted and abnormal returns from investing in the buy-side firm and eighty-five sell-side firms' buy recommendations from July 1997 to December 2004.

	Buy-side firm (percentage)	Sell-side firms
Market-adjusted returns		
Mean	2.3%	8.2%*
Median	2.3	7.4*
Buy-side firm percentile rank	12	
Abnormal returns		
Mean	2.3	6.1*
Median	2.3	5.3*
Buy-side firm percentile rank	24	

*Significantly different from zero and from the buy-side performance at the 1 percent level.

NOTE: Market-adjusted returns were the difference between the holding period return for a buy- or sell-side firm's recommendation portfolio and the return on the value-weighted S&P 500 market index. Abnormal returns were computed for each firm's recommendation portfolio by regressing its portfolio returns on the market excess return, a zero-investment-size portfolio return, a zero-investment book-to-market portfolio return and a zero-investment price momentum portfolio return. To create the firm portfolios, we bought and held all stocks rated by a firm as a strong buy or buy from the day after the initial rating until the day after they were downgraded to a hold or lower rating (if they continued to be covered) or for 250 days (if they ceased to be covered).

SOURCE: Boris Groysberg, Paul Healy, George Serafeim, and Devin Shanthikumar, "The Stock Selection and Performance of Buy-Side Analysts," *Management Science* (forthcoming).

Abnormal return results also show sell-side firms outperformed the buy-side firm. The annualized abnormal return from investing in strong buy/buy recommendations issued by the buy-side firm analysts' is 2.3 percent, versus 6.1 percent for those issued by the average sell-side firm. Median sell-side firm abnormal return was 5.3 percent, also significantly higher than the buy-side firm return. The buy-side firm was ranked at the twenty-fourth percentile relative to sell-side firms.

Why Do Sell-Side Buy Recommendations Outperform?

The analysts at the buy-side firm covered less volatile and higher market cap stocks than their sell-side peers. After controlling for these differences, most notably the difference in market cap of stocks covered, the performance of the sell-side analysts' strong buy/buy recommendations is essentially the same as that of the buy-side firm analysts. To demonstrate this effect, we compare market-adjusted and abnormal returns for strong buy/buy recommendations for four subsets of companies: (1) those with recommendations issued by both buy- and sell-side analysts; (2) those for which the only recommendations are issued by sell-side analysts; (3) those with large market capitalizations for which the only recommendations are issued by sell-side analysts; and (4) those with small market capitalizations for which the only recommendations are issued by sell-side analysts. Firms are classified as having small (large) market caps if their average capitalization is lower than or equal to (higher than) the median firm recommended by sell-side firms.

The findings are reported in Exhibit 6.8. For companies with recommendations issued by both buy- and sell-side analysts, the mean market-adjusted returns for strong buy/buy recommendations are 2.3 percent for buy-side analysts and 3.2 percent for their sell-side peers. Abnormal returns for the same portfolios are 2.3 percent and 3.05 percent respectively and statistically indistinguishable. Interestingly, mean market-adjusted (10.2 percent) and abnormal (8.1 percent) returns for strong buy/buy recommendations issued for companies covered only by the sell-side are economically and statistically important. These findings suggest that much of the outperformance of sell-side analysts comes from selecting stocks not recommended by their buy-side peers.

Classifying recommendations for companies covered only by sell-side analysts into those for small and large companies reinforces the findings described in the previous paragraphs and indicates that the superior

Exhibit 6.8 Market-adjusted and abnormal returns from investing in subsamples of analysts strong buy/buy recommendations for sell-side analysts' for the period July 1997 to December 2004.

	Market-adjusted return		Abnormal return	
Subsample	Mean (percentage)	Median (percentage)	Mean (percentage)	Median (percentage)
Sell-side returns for:				
Firms covered by both the buy and sell sides	3.20%	2.80%	3.05%	3.10%
Firms covered only by the sell side	10.20*	9.90*	8.10*	7.60*
Difference	(7.00)*	(7.10)*	(5.05)*	(4.50)*
Large firms covered only by the sell side	5.00*	4.80*	4.70*	4.60*
Small firms covered only by the sell side	12.30*	10.90*	11.40*	9.10*
Difference	(7.30)*	(6.10)*	(6.70)*	(4.50)*
Buy-side returns for:				
Firms covered by both the buy and sell sides	2.30		2.30	

*Significantly different from zero at the 5 percent level.

NOTE: Market-adjusted returns were the difference between the holding period return for a buy- or sell-side firm's recommendation portfolio and the return on the value-weighted S&P 500 market index. Abnormal returns were computed for each firm's recommendation portfolio by regressing its portfolio returns on the market excess return, a zero-investment size portfolio return, a zero investment book-to-market portfolio return and a zero investment price momentum portfolio return. To create the firm portfolios, we bought and held all stocks rated by a firm as a Strong Buy or Buy from the day after the initial rating until the day after they were downgraded to a Hold or lower rating (if they continued to be covered), or for 250 days (if they ceased to be covered).

SOURCE: Boris Groysberg, Paul Healy, George Serafeim, and Devin Shanthikumar, "The Stock Selection and Performance of Buy-Side Analysts," *Management Science* (forthcoming).

performance of sell-side analysts strong buy/buy recommendations emanates largely from their exclusive coverage of small companies. The mean market-adjusted return to sell-side analysts' strong buy/buy recommendations for small stocks not covered by the buy side is 12.3 percent versus 5.0 percent for large stock recommendations. Mean abnormal returns for these two portfolios, which control for the well-documented firm size effect on returns, are 11.4 percent and 4.7 percent respectively. The small versus large company differences are statistically reliable as well as economically material.

In summary, much of the outperformance of sell-side analysts' strong buy/buy recommendations appears to come from their coverage of some small stocks, presumably potential or former banking clients. These firms generate strong returns but are unattractive to buy-side firms that demand liquidity. Sell-side analysts recommend smaller stocks, perhaps because these firms are clients.

How Generalizable Are the Results?

One limitation of our research is that our buy-side analyst sample is from a single firm, raising questions about whether the findings are applicable to other investment firms. To help answer this question, we obtained recommendations for buy- and sell-side analysts from two surveys we conducted in 2005 and 2006. The surveys requested more than 5,000 analysts to provide us anonymously with recommendations for three large market cap stocks that they covered from a list of companies in the industries they indicated they covered. We included only companies listed on the major stock indices. In the United States, for example, only companies listed on the S&P 500 Index were included. We received responses from 967 analysts, representing a 19 percent response rate. The U.S. sample included 432 sell-side analysts who issued 1,202 strong buy/buy recommendations and 100 buy-side analysts who provided 282 strong buy/buy recommendations.

The mean market cap of stocks recommended by buy-side analysts was $30.7 billion versus $27.6 billion for those recommended by the sell side, implying that the recommended stocks for the two subsamples have similar size/liquidity. As reported in Exhibit 6.9, the average market-adjusted strong buy/buy recommendation return (for 250 days from the date of the survey response) is 1.4 percent for the survey buy-side analysts versus 2.3 percent for the sell-side analysts. Comparable mean abnormal returns are 3.2 percent for buy-side analysts and 3.0 percent for sell-side peers. These findings are remarkably similar to those reported in the preceding paragraphs and indicate that, at least after controlling for differences in the size of firms recommended, sell-side analysts show comparable performance to their buy-side peers.

Exhibit 6.9 Performance of buy and sell-side analyst strong buy/buy recommendations collected from analyst survey.

	Buy-side analysts	Sell-side analysts	Difference
Mean returns			
Market-adjusted	1.4%	2.3%	(0.9)%
Abnormal	3.2%	3.0%	0.2%
Number of recommendations	282	1,202	
Number of analysts	100	432	
Average market capitalization	$30.7 billion	$27.6 billion	

NOTE: Market-adjusted returns are the difference between the holding period return for a buy- or sell-side firm's recommendation portfolio and the return on the value-weighted S&P 500 market index. Abnormal returns were computed for each firm's recommendation portfolio by regressing its portfolio returns on the market excess return, a zero-investment size portfolio return, a zero-investment book-to-market portfolio return, and a zero-investment price momentum portfolio return. To create the firm portfolios, we bought and held all stocks rated by a firm as a strong buy or buy for 250 days beginning on the date of the survey response.

SOURCE: Boris Groysberg, Paul Healy, George Serafeim, and Devin Shanthikumar, "The Stock Selection and Performance of Buy-Side Analysts," *Management Science* (forthcoming).

Conclusions

The performance of sell-side analysts has been a topic of popular discussion in recent years with particular concern raised over investment banking conflicts of interest. The use of investment banking to fund equity research certainly appeared to influence some well-known sell-side analysts during the height of the tech stock boom. But the exclusive focus on banking conflicts ignores other possible conflicts, notably the brokerage conflict that arises from funding research through brokerage commissions.

The evidence provided in this chapter suggests that brokerage conflicts of interest are at least as significant as those attributable to investment banking. Prior to the Global Settlement, analysts at firms that supported research exclusively through their brokerage business issued more optimistic earnings and price estimates than analysts at full-service investment banks. Two factors appear to explain this finding. First, analysts at high-status firms, such as the bulge-bracket investment banks, were better able to resist attracting business through optimistic research. Second, brokerage firms with retail clients were particularly susceptible to providing optimistic research.

Further evidence even questions whether conflicts of interest are of first-order importance for research quality. In a study that compares the performance of analysts at a large prestigious buy-side firm and their sell-side peers, we find that the sell-side analysts issued more accurate and less optimistic earnings estimates and made stock recommendations that were at least as profitable as the buy-side firm peers. Yet analysts at the buy-side firm faced no incentives to overstate their research to generate investment banking or brokerage business, and they did not have to worry about how their conclusions affected future access to company managers.

The strong performance of the sell-side underscores two core industry strengths: intense competition and transparency of analyst performance. Clients regularly rate sell-side analysts on the quality of their research. This information is widely available and is used as a basis for determining sell-side bonuses, making it difficult for unsuccessful analysts to survive. As a former *Institutional Investor*-ranked insurance analyst argued, "Well, if you lose money for clients, if you tell them to buy a stock and it goes down 40 percent, if you do that too many times they're not going to listen to you anymore! And then you're out." In contrast, at least until recently, many buy-side firms have been less competitive and have not used relative performance benchmarks for their analysts, enabling lower-performing analysts to survive longer. This might be changing as buy-side firms focus on increasing the value of their own research and using services such as StarMine to benchmark their analysts against analysts at other buy-side firms and the sell side. It remains to be seen how these changes will influence the quality of buy-side research.

7

The Future of Sell-Side Research
in the United States

At this stage, you may have concluded that the sell-side research industry's best days are over and that the industry is mature or even in decline. Regulatory changes, technological advancements, increased access to information, and the growing sophistication and diversity of buy-side customers appear to have adversely affected the industry's economic prospects. Indeed, many of our colleagues have questioned why we would want to write a book on an industry they consider stagnant or declining.

Yet, as history has shown, the industry has been remarkably resilient and innovative. Our study of Prudential showed how, in response to the emergence of the investment banking model for funding research, the company built an investment banking business for midmarket firms. In anticipation of the concern over banking conflicts of interest and regulatory action, it subsequently exited investment banking and focused on providing brokerage services that better served its clients' interests. Today many of the remaining U.S. sell-side firms continue to innovate in response to the structural changes discussed in this book, and to the weakened economies in the United States and Western Europe.

In this chapter, we examine U.S. buy-side clients' ongoing demand for sell-side research and report on a variety of innovations undertaken by U.S. firms to increase the value of their services as they respond to the challenges. In Chapter 8, we discuss new opportunities for the industry that have arisen in rapidly growing emerging markets, where spending on sell-side research continues to grow.

Buy-Side Perspectives

A recent survey reported that large asset managers rate sell-side research as low in value and that 70 percent believe they overpay for it, whereas investment managers at midsize firms are more satisfied.[1] This is ominous news for sell-side research departments because the large investment firms surveyed provide the bulk of their funding. Yet, given the large number of money management firms and hedge funds that use sell-side research and the modest size of even the largest buy-side research departments, it is uneconomic for institutional investors to replicate the analysis performed by the sell side. Additionally, buy-side analysts and portfolio managers may view it as in their interest to downplay the contributions of sell-side research to their investment process. As one sell-side research department manager explained:

> If you're a large buy-side firm and you're trying to appeal to pension funds, you want to say, "Look, I have proprietary research. I do my own research. I don't rely on Street research, that's generic. We come up with our own insights." But the reality is that our biggest consumers are these large shops that claim to have their own research houses.

To better understand the role of sell-side research, we conducted field studies at two large asset management firms, a regional firm (Morgan Asset Management), and several hedge funds.

Views of Large Asset Management Firms

Our two research sites were among the largest asset management firms in the United States. Each had more than $100 billion of assets under management, employed more than forty research analysts, and had doubled the size of their internal research departments over the prior eight years. Interviews with the research directors at the two firms revealed subtle differences in the ways that each organized its own analysts, but both continued to see sell-side research as a fundamental input into their decision making.

In explaining the decision to expand its internal research capabilities so significantly, the research manager at the first firm explained that it grew out of recognition in the early 2000s of the challenges to momentum and growth strategies that had dominated the 1990s. Regulation Fair Disclosure deterred company managers from providing favored sell-side analysts with guidance on short-term earnings news, a key to momentum investing success, and the end of the technology boom had made investors jittery about growth funds. As a result, the firm began exploring value investing opportunities. Value investments had a longer horizon than the quarter-to-quarter focus of most sell-side analysts, and led to the decision to hire more in-house analysts who could be trained to better meet the firm's research needs.

The growth of internal research was accompanied by a change in the way the firm's research analysts were developed. Formerly, when they joined the firm analysts learned about and covered an industry. Those who were successful were quickly promoted to portfolio managers, where general rather than focused knowledge was critical. However, this meant that there was high turnover among research analysts, affecting the quality of their work. The firm therefore decided to provide career opportunities for analysts in its research department. Analysts became investors in focused funds and in rare cases could become portfolio managers. But most continued to work in research, building experience in covering their industries.

The increased number of in-house analysts and the higher quality of their research reduced resources allocated to sell-side research. This arose naturally from declining commission rates, but the research director noted that his firm had also concentrated trading volume among fewer sell-side firms, allowing it to negotiate even lower commission rates.

Nonetheless, analysts and portfolio managers at the firm continue to value sell-side analysts' research. And they conduct regular broker votes, along the lines of those described in Chapter 3. For each quarter they allocate points to those sell-side analysts whose research has been most important. The aggregated votes are then used to allocate the next quarter's trading commissions across firms. Sell-side analysts' depth of knowledge on an industry and companies they cover (which are far fewer than those covered by the average in-house analyst) continues to be valued. The sell-side analysts' ability to arrange meetings with senior corporate managers at sell-side sponsored conferences is also important. Given its size, the asset management firm can arrange its own meetings with corporate managers. But sell-side conferences that attract many key corporate CEOs in an industry provide its buy-side analysts and portfolio managers with an efficient way to organize these meetings. Finally, the sell-side firms are perceived to create value by providing opportunities for the firms' portfolio managers to participate in new issues.

One opportunity for sell-side firms, identified by the research manager at the asset-management firm, is providing clients with a global perspective on stocks and industries. Analysts at the money management firm, and also at most sell-side firms, specialize in industries within a geographic region (such as United States, Asia-Pacific, and Europe). Geographic specialization ensures that analysts understand common accounting, regulatory, market, and cultural factors that affect the firms they covered. But, as a result, no one analyst has the knowledge required to evaluate the best investment opportunities within a global industry. The challenge of summarizing research from multiple analysts is exacerbated because analysts in different regions frequently use different models and frameworks. Despite increased demand for this type of advice, the research manager observed that even leading investment banks that attempt to provide this type of advice are not very successful.

The second large asset management firm that we interviewed has chosen a somewhat differentiated approach to the organization of its research department. Rather than setting up a centralized research department that services all portfolio managers in the firm, it has structured itself as a "multiboutique firm." Analysts are organized into four teams, with each focused on a handful of related product mandates (for example, value investments). The analysts on a given team work solely with the portfolio managers on that team. This permits analysts to provide portfolio managers on their team with tailored, relevant research that is consistent with the fund's philosophy. In describing the approach, the firm's equities director observed, "If you have a centralized research group that is feeding into portfolio managers who have very different investment philosophies, that's a tough task for an analyst." The small group setting also maximizes creativity and idea generation.

Despite the increased importance of its own research department, the research manager at the asset management firm acknowledged that sell-side firms continue to add value. Bulge-bracket sell-side firms contribute through the management access they provide via conferences, field trips, and one-on-one meetings. As one portfolio manager at the firm observed, there is no material difference in research quality for bulge-bracket and the midsized/regional firms, but bulge firms differentiate themselves by their ability to provide clients with management access. The firm's equities director argued that independent firms also add important "pieces to the puzzle" through "really in-depth research on a narrow topic." These contributions are rewarded in the way the asset management firm allocates future commissions to sell-side firms via semiannual buy-side analyst and portfolio manager votes.

View from a Regional Asset Management Firm

Headquartered in Birmingham, Alabama, Morgan Asset Management, Inc. (MAM), markets itself as an active, diversified, long-term, high-quality investment manager.[2] As of March 31, 2010, the firm managed $25.0 billion in institutional and personal trust accounts; employed ten analysts, seventy-one portfolio managers and five traders; and had offices in sixteen states.

MAM's equity research department includes six sector-focused equity analysts and a director of equity research. Most research analysts at the firm had passed, or were working toward, CFA accreditation. Many had graduate degrees in finance; some had CPAs. The analysts tended to have a background in finance rather than industry, and sector coverage decisions were generally made on the basis of the analyst's interests and prior experience. Each was responsible for covering approximately seventy to ninety stocks in one or two industries.

Not surprisingly, given its relatively small equity research department, MAM's analysts rely heavily on sell-side research. Financial models are viewed as a particularly valuable sell-side tool. One analyst commented, "They [the sell side] are a lot better equipped to do complicated earnings models."[3] MAM analysts also use the sell side as a sounding board to provide additional opinions. A research manager explained, "One thing that I like to do . . . is to get as many opinions as possible, and there are no bad opinions."[4] Finally, MAM analysts and portfolio managers cited corporate access as a key service provided by the sell side.

Despite the value that MAM places on sell-side research, declining resources put pressure on its demand for sell-side research. Guillermo Araoz, director of equity research for MAM, explained:

> Our falling budget is forcing us to choose between sell-side research and raw data. Here are the options. First, allow the budget cuts to fall primarily on sell-side research. In this course of action, we limit our access to

sell-side experts and company management. We receive fewer company forecasts and less industry-specific information. Given that we only have six analysts each covering about 80 stocks, we really need the sell side to give us granular information about companies. . . . The second option is to allow the budget cuts to fall primarily on data vendors (Bloomberg and FactSet). In this course of action, we receive less market data, limiting our ability to conduct backtesting on models, and to access international macro and U.S. data. So far, I have cut research services of those sell-side firms that cover the least number of companies. I want to keep as much breadth of coverage from the sell side as possible.[5]

Another challenge for MAM's research analysts is that sell-side firms increasingly restrict access to information and services, including conferences and management road shows, for clients with lower commission payments. Given MAM's relatively small size, such decisions can jeopardize its access to sell-side research.

Hedge Fund Views on Sell-Side Research

To understand how hedge funds utilize sell-side research and have affected sell-side research, we interviewed portfolio managers at a number of hedge funds and sell-side research managers. These interviews reveal that hedge funds value many of the same elements of the sell-side research product as traditional asset managers. For example, one hedge fund manager confirmed that the sell side's access to management is especially valuable for his firm because it is uneconomic for hedge funds to organize one-on-one meetings and conferences with management. Strong written research and models are also important, she observed, but only as a starting point. "You couldn't get to first base with us if you didn't have those, but that isn't enough to stand out," she said.

Sell-side analysts' influence over the investment debate and in moving markets is also a primary reason that hedge fund analysts and portfolio managers use sell-side research. One hedge fund manager explained, "We pay a lot of attention to sell-side research. It is essential that we know and understand where the sell side is on any stock we really care about as it helps us to understand where the market is." She added, "We use the sell side as an input. We use it to benchmark our own conclusions but we aren't relying on the sell side for research."

A number of hedge fund managers also highlighted the importance of the nonresearch services provided by the sell side. For example, large sell-side firms, such as Goldman Sachs, regularly host conferences where they invite hedge funds to make presentations to an audience of large potential investors. After the presentations, the speakers have one-on-one meetings with audience members to provide more information about their funds. These conferences serve as a marketing tool for hedge funds looking for investors and are also useful for fund-of-fund managers looking for new investments.

Sell-side firms also function as "prime brokers" for hedge funds. Teena Lerner of Rx Capital, a health care hedge fund, explained the importance of this role:

> Not only do they hold your securities and lend you money for the short selling, but they provide you with many other services to ensure that they keep your business. They help you set up the hedge fund, find office space, market the business, and introduce you to vendors, and help with information technology outsourcing, hiring, and fundraising. They also help on an ongoing basis with all sorts of useful data and reports that aid in managing the portfolio. Their business model is one where they offer services to start-up funds before they see any revenue, so they are very selective as to whom they want to get involved with initially. Goldman Sachs and Morgan Stanley were both doing things for me before they had a commitment from my business. It was unbelievable and very helpful, as I was new to the operations side.[6]

In part because of the wide range of services that hedge funds receive from sell-side firms, they have generally paid trade commission rates at the high end of the range. According to Greenwich Associates, hedge funds comprised 25 to 30 percent of total commissions as of 2009.[7] In allocating commissions between sell-side firms, many hedge funds conduct a broker vote, although the process is often less formal than the votes conducted at larger buy-side firms. Hedge fund analysts, portfolio managers, and traders weigh in on which firms they find the most helpful, establishing commission allocation targets. Traders do their best to manage to these targets in allocating trades.

The interviews also revealed several factors that limit hedge fund demand for sell-side research. First, although research-focused funds tend to be heavy users of sell-side research, quantitative funds typically have little use for sell-side research.

Second, the short investment horizon of many hedge funds can reduce the relevance of traditional written stock research and recommendations. One sell–side manager observed that because hedge funds "have such a short window of performance expectations, they tend to focus only on what is going to happen next quarter, and ignore a stock's long term investment value." Another sell–side manager observed that "a lot goes on with hedge funds on a day-to-day basis that requires a very nimble response to events. The time required for an analyst to process a piece of information, get it through compliance and then get it out and meet the global dissemination rules, can hinder your ability to fully support hedge fund clients who want access to the information immediately."

Finally, the multiasset, long/short strategies employed by hedge funds and their absolute return benchmarks are typically not a good fit with traditional sell–side research, which focuses primarily on long-only equity investment ideas where investment performance is measured by outperforming the S&P 500. To better serve hedge fund clients, some sell–side firms have begun producing cross–asset class research reports (see our discussion of Merrill Lynch in the following pages).

In summary, despite efforts by large asset management firms and hedge funds to develop proprietary investment knowledge through in-house research, sell–side research continues to have value for many of these clients. Sell–side conferences and access to management are consistently rated as valuable, either because they are an efficient way for buy–side analysts and portfolio managers to meet company executives or because sell–side analysts can provide access that would otherwise be difficult to obtain. Sell–side analysts' industry knowledge and understanding of market perceptions are also considered important to many buy–side clients.

Sell-Side Firm Innovations

Our interviews of research directors at a broad range of sell–side firms reveal a number of innovations generated to address the industry's strategic challenges and the impacts of rapidly evolving technology and the new regulatory environment.

BofA Merrill Lynch

In response to the emergence of hedge funds and increased globalization, the research department at BofA Merrill Lynch (ML) has made a number of changes in the way it conducts, aggregates, and distributes its research.[8]

To address the growing hedge fund client segment, the bank's research department has focused on "capital structure collaboration" and introduced a number of research products targeted specifically at hedge funds. In December 2002, ML produced the first in a series of cross-asset class industry reports, "The Cable Industry Capital-Structure Monitor." The ninety-six-page report combined the ideas of analysts in equity, high-grade fixed income, high-yield, and convertible research. The idea for such a report emanated from ML's own sales force assessment of the type of research sought by hedge fund clients. It was well received. Analyst Jessica Reif Cohen commented, "We got great client feedback . . . and because it was the first report of its kind, Merrill made a big marketing push. We had an internal sales-force presentation, and the analysts did a couple of joint meetings. And it was really marketed by Merrill Lynch as a firm."[9]

Subsequent such reports included "Capital Structure Investing in Utilities" (April 2003) and "Capital Structure Investing in Autos" (November 2003). The auto report covered not only multiple asset classes but also multiple geographies. Analysts from London and New York were involved, and the overall team totaled twenty-three analysts. U.S. auto analyst John Casesa recounted one of the report's findings:

> Because we had followed GM and Fiat and they had a relationship, we were able to articulate strategies for GM and Fiat convertibles and hedge positions between GM and Fiat securities. We also pointed out that it made more sense to be a bondholder of GM than a stockholder, and to be a holder of the finance company's bonds than the parent company's bonds. And we outlined some derivative strategies that would allow investors to hedge their positions across asset classes by bringing all of our bond and stock opinions together.[10]

ML also established joint ventures between different parts of its trading and research business with the goal of producing such cross-asset reports on a regular basis. The Distressed Equity Desk was created as a joint venture between Equities and Fixed Income. Its purpose is to identify trading opportunities that arose as a result of financial distress. And its Desk Intelligence report provides short-term trading ideas, such as "Buy XYZ September $50 Calls, Sell XYZ September $40 Puts."

ML has launched similar initiatives to promote research reports that are global rather than country based or regional. In 2000–2001, it began appointing mangers to integrate regional research coverage and produce sector-based reports that transcended geographic boundaries. It has since launched a series of regular research reports with a global focus, some of which also have a cross-asset investment approach. For example, its weekly Global Research Highlights report provides "a streamlined collection of the very best ideas and thought-provoking research across multiple disciplines—economics, investment strategy, fundamental equity, fixed income, currencies and commodities."[11]

Credit Suisse

Research continues to be an important element of Credit Suisse's (CS's) strategy.[12] To drive its analysts' focus on meeting customer needs and to increase the financial contribution of research, CS has transformed its research department into a profit center. This change has enabled the firm to measure the profitability of each analyst and each customer. Analysts are rewarded on the basis of profitability, motivating them to assess how to better meet the needs of each customer and to segment accounts based on their financial contribution.

To measure research profitability, CS has developed a methodology for estimating the revenues generated by its research department that stands up to the scrutiny of its research analysts, salesmen, and traders—no easy task. Commission revenues cover trade execution costs and compensate firms for their research and sales services. Because customers do not value each component separately, traders and salesmen argue that the lion's share of commissions earned are attributable to their sales and trading efforts, whereas research personnel are equally convinced that research is the critical driver. Their disagreements have been further complicated by wide dispersion in commission rates, from as low as one cent per share for electronic trades to nearly four cents for a full-service trade. As a result, research departments have typically been treated as cost centers, undermining their importance in the highly profit-focused world of investment banking.

CS recognized that polls of buy-side portfolio managers and analysts could provide a useful way of quantifying its research department revenues. For example, in a 2003 *Institutional Investor* poll, buy-side firms were asked to rate the relative importance of research, sales, and trading in allocating commissions. Investment professionals at the firms judged that 57 percent of commission dollars were attributable to research, 18 percent to sales, and 25 percent to trading, whereas the firms' traders allocated 41 percent to research, 9 percent to sales, and 50 percent to trading.[13] A similar buy-side poll conducted by Greenwich Associates found that 38 to 39 percent of commissions were viewed as compensation for research services.[14]

In explaining how these results were used to estimate research revenues at Credit Suisse, Stefano Natella (global research head) commented,

> You are never going to nail down the [exact] number. The number changes from account to account and by region . . . we don't know if it's 40 percent, 35 percent, 30 percent, 25 percent. We think that probably the right range is somewhere between 25 percent and 40 percent . . . Let's run research so that we break even at 25 percent of secondary commissions. . . . use the lowest part of the range, where everybody agrees.[15]

Managers at CS decided to assume that 25 percent of trading revenues were attributable to the research department. As a further refinement, Natella determined that only 50 percent of algorithmic/electronic trading commissions would be included in the calculation. He explained, "We made an assumption that 50% of the firms that are trading electronically are not trading electronically to pay for research, they are trading electronically because it is a cheaper way of doing it."[16]

Roughly 75 percent of direct departmental costs, such as personnel, production, legal, and compliance costs, were allocated to the research department with the remainder allocated to other divisions that used analyst research services, such as investment banking and M&A. Combining the revenues and allocated costs generated a research department profit and loss (P&L).

CS did not stop there. It generated P&Ls for each analyst. The emergence of third-party services, such as TheMarkets.com's MeritMark, to manage the buy-side vote aggregation process increased the number of buy-side firms reporting broker votes to sell-side firms. By 2003, 60 to 70 percent of CS's clients provided feedback for each of its analysts.[17] This enabled CS to estimate analyst revenues and P&Ls. Research department revenues for each client were allocated to specific analysts based on the percentage of the clients' votes they received. For example, if a buy-side firm generated $25 million in revenues for the research department in 2003 and awarded CS a total of 100 broker votes, an analyst who received ten of those votes would be allocated $2.5 million of revenues ($25 million [10/100]). By repeating this procedure for each client and allocating the direct and a share of indirect costs to each analyst, Credit Suisse was able to construct P&Ls for each of its analysts.

To ensure that analysts took responsibility for their P&Ls, CS based 70 to 80 percent of the annual bonuses on individual analyst profitability. Managers had discretion to determine the remainder based on analysts' contributions to non–revenue-producing activities (such as participation in firm training programs) and to deal with exceptions (for example, to give new analysts time to prove themselves). Look again at Exhibits 2.6 and 2.7 for more details on Credit Suisse's analyst P&Ls.

The approach generated dramatic improvement in CS's research department profitability (from a loss to a healthy profit) and reduced the cost per stock covered. By understanding more about their best clients, notably which particular services they valued and which they did not, CS's analysts were able to improve their value added. The new approach also encouraged analysts to think carefully about expenses associated with everything from hiring junior analysts to acquiring new databases and travel. As John McNulty, a basic materials analyst, recalled:

> In the past, where I really focused was on the [loss] side. For a long time, I had one associate, didn't travel as much as I should have, and cut back on data sources that realistically I needed to have. But when you start to actually do the math, and figure out, "what's the leverage in getting three incremental votes in terms of what does it mean on the revenue side," it pretty quickly offsets the cost side . . . it's a really leverageable system.[18]

In 2006, CS took its approach one step further by measuring customer profitability and segmenting clients on this basis. Clients were segmented into five categories, and research managers directed analysts and salespeople to service the clients differentially:

1. *High-Touch.* Approximately eighty high-priority clients for whom analysts and salespeople provide full services.
2. *Sales Managed Content.* Analysts work with the salespeople to understand which services these clients value and which they can afford. The 150 or so accounts in this category are separated into two categories, roughly twenty accounts whose priority is management access and those with the potential to become high-touch clients.
3. *Management Access.* Roughly twenty clients whose priority is management access, allowing service to be tailored accordingly.
4. *Growth Opportunity.* Clients who are viewed as having the potential to become high-touch clients.

5. *Institutional Markets.* The vast majority of clients, which pay lower commissions and which are further segmented into A, B, C, D grades based on commission revenues they generate.[19]

The research director at CS noted that these changes had enabled the firm to increase the quality of its research offerings by identifying those services that its clients valued most highly and to segment its services by providing a full menu of services to its most profitable clients and limiting the menu offered to those that were less profitable or were perceived to have less profit potential.

Sanford C. Bernstein

Sanford C. Bernstein (Bernstein) is a leading brokerage firm and asset manager with a reputation for rigorous, in-depth, highly quantitative, and independent sell-side investment research.[20] The firm's Institutional Research Services (IRS) division provides investment research and trading services to professional money management firms. In 2008, IRS had more than ninety research professionals, including nearly thirty senior analysts, located in New York, Los Angeles, and London.

A critical source of Bernstein's success emanates from the reputation of its sell-side research, epitomized by its trademark product, the Black Book. These dense research reports, bound in a black cover, provide in-depth analysis on a specific topic, company, or investment thesis. Lisa Shalett, an executive vice president at Bernstein, described the Bernstein sell-side research product as follows:

> The difference with our reports is that we're trying to conduct analyses for sophisticated investors—to recommend and report to readers that understand the subject very well. . . . We're trying to do something different . . . We focus on the fundamentals and the long term versus near-term maintenance and news.[21]

A former Global Director of Research at Bernstein, added:

> We go to a level of depth that others may not be willing or may not have the time to go to. We try and bring a level of expertise and industry knowledge to the challenge of investing that others may not have.

Because it does not have an investment banking practice, Bernstein's sell-side research is free from investment banking conflicts. Among the firms ranked in the top ten of *Institutional Investor*'s 2008 All-America Research team, Bernstein is the only one without an investment banking division. Perhaps as a result, its research has a reputation for being independent and anticonsensus. Vladimir Zlotnikov, a Bernstein analyst, opined:

> If after spending several months of research you come back with a consensus view, you shouldn't publish it. As a reader, why would I invest half an hour of my time if I find a conclusion that is identical to something I already knew? As little time as possible should be devoted to understanding and compiling the consensus view, and most of the time should be spent on trying to figure out how the reality is likely to be different.[22]

To provide a high-quality research product, Bernstein devotes considerable resources to hiring, training, and evaluating the performance of its analysts. The firm has traditionally hired new analysts from the outside. But, in contrast to most competitors, it has focused on candidates with backgrounds in the industries they will cover rather than experienced analysts or recent MBAs. However, in recent years, it has also promoted associates from within the firm. Bernstein recruits associates, who provide support for senior analysts, from MBA and undergraduate programs. Its associate program has been restructured to ensure that junior analysts are being appropriately trained and developed. As a result, approximately 20 percent of current analysts were formerly associates with the firm.

Candidates for analyst positions at Bernstein are expected to have strong intellectual capabilities and character traits rather than a specific background or knowledge base. Lisa Shalett observed:

> You need to be incredibly bright and analytical. You need to be fascinated with numbers, and you have to be a good communicator and have some type of charisma and marketing savvy. What you really need is to be insatiably curious, unbelievably competitive and want to win. You've got to have a willingness to be bold and sometimes say something that is different, and willing to argue about what you believe and have the courage of your convictions. And you also have to be intellectually and professionally resilient in the sense that you're going to publish, and you're going to be out there, and you're going to be wrong in public.[23]

The process of hiring a new senior analyst costs an estimated $500,000 to $1,000,000.[24] Headhunters help to identify initial candidates from industry and the firm screens 100 resumes and interviews forty to fifty people. Before being offered a position, a candidate interviews with twenty or more Bernstein employees.

Once hired, the new analyst is typically trained for a full year, study-
ing the industry, learning the Bernstein culture by reading Bernstein research and interacting with experienced analysts, and meeting regularly
with the research director to discuss progress. Classes and other formal
training fill in knowledge gaps as necessary. Sallie Krawcheck, former
CEO of Bernstein, explained how this process works:

> One analyst—Scott Hill, who covers autos and auto parts, a phenomenally
> intelligent guy—is a lawyer by training. He has a wonderful demographic
> theory on the auto companies. But being a lawyer, when he got here, he'd
> never heard of a discounted cash-flow statement or a PE. So Scott's train-
> ing was very much Finance 101, Economics 101, Equity Research 101.
> Then there's Toni Sacconaghi, one of our consulting hires. He's a finance
> whiz, and a very analytical guy. Toni needed something quite different,
> and we were able to guide him through what our investors care about. So
> it tends to be a very individualized type of process for everybody.[25]

To evaluate the performance of its analysts, Bernstein relies increasingly
on feedback from buy-side client votes, internal sales people and traders,
and external polls (such as Greenwich or *Institutional Investor*). These data
are used to compute a "market traction" score for an analyst, which is the
primary driver of compensation. Additionally, management tracks a variety
of statistics that correlate highly with the market traction score, including
time spent on the phone and in person with clients, and the frequency with
which an analyst publishes proactive research. Bernstein discloses these statistics to its analysts on a quarterly basis to help them learn how to improve
their performance.

Because Bernstein does not have an investment banking business, it relies almost exclusively on trade commissions to fund its sell-side research
business. In recent years, Bernstein has invested heavily to improve the
capabilities of its trading platform, adding traders and increasing trading
services, including sophisticated algorithmic trade offerings. Bernstein
management has also focused on monitoring trade commissions and resource consumption on a client-by-client basis to ensure that the two are
broadly aligned and that buy-side clients are paying for the resources they
receive. A Bernstein research executive explained how clients are managed:

> We now keep track of where we are: where our resources are being de-
> voted, what our revenues are, how they align. And we try to address the
> places where these don't really line up. For example, let's say I've got a

client that is #15 in terms of resource consumption but #50 in terms of where we're being paid. That leads to a discussion with that client about finding a way to get those numbers better aligned . . . Or we may have to tell the client "you really can't have access to these analysts, given what we're doing here," or "you really can't expect to be attending this partic-ular conference, given where we are from a business standpoint" . . . Sim-ilarly, if the numbers are reversed, we understand that the situation . . . is unlikely to be sustainable in the long term, and we need to do some-thing about that as well.

Sidoti & Company

Formed in March 1999 by Peter Sidoti, Sidoti & Company, LLC (Sidoti) provides institutional investors with research and management access for micro-, small-, and midcap stocks with an equity market value of $3 bil-lion or less.[26] Clients are buy-side analysts and portfolio managers at small and midcap institutions, typically long-only investment firms. Hedge funds represent only 10 percent of its business. By 2012, Sidoti employed over seventy analysts who wrote reports on more than 900 small-cap and microcap companies in more than thirty industry sectors. The company aims to expand stock coverage to 700 small-cap equities and 600 micro-caps by the end of 2013.[27]

In discussing future growth opportunities, founder Peter Sidoti an-ticipated partnering with bulge-bracket firms that lack small-cap research expertise:

> We've been approached by a couple of the larger firms where they want to do the investment banking and pay us to do the research for the smaller-cap names. So over the next two or three years, the business is going to evolve . . . I can see where we will end up doing the research for two or three investment banking firms. The bankers don't want to do the research. They have no interest in the research side of this market. They don't have the critical mass to work in the small-cap arena. That's all we do. So, the idea to pay us to do the work just makes sense.

Three aspects of Sidoti's research strategy are distinctive. First, its analysts focus on microcap (since 2010), small, and midcap stocks that are not widely covered by its competitors. Peter Sidoti recalled, "When the firm started, we deliberately chose not to compete with the bulge-bracket firms. If a small- or midcap stock was already being covered by two or more bulge-bracket firms, we would not pick up coverage." However, in Sidoti's view, this changed as Reg FD reduced the edge that strong corporate relationships provided to the largest firms and as the quality of small-cap research deteriorated.

Second, in its decision not to pursue investment banking, Sidoti sought to increase clients' confidence in the integrity of the firm's research:

> We are aware of no other firm in our niche with few ties to investment banking. The oldest independent research groups—the Value Line Survey and Argus Research—focus on large-cap stocks and do not provide institutional-quality product. Sanford Bernstein . . . focuses only on the large end of the market.
>
> Some large wire houses have special sales and trading teams focused on equities with relatively small market caps; their efforts, however, are small and not coordinated well with the research teams of the firms. The research departments, meanwhile, appear in disarray. Scandals and a host of new rules and limits pose higher hurdles for the analysts.[28]

Finally, Sidoti provides clients with a high level of access to corporate management of firms it covers. In 2009, the firm sponsored 900 management road show days and approximately 200 management conference calls. They also hosted three large annual conferences, two in New York and one in San Francisco, at which management teams presented to institutional investor clients. For some clients, Sidoti's ability to provide corporate access was their primary reason for doing business with the firm. As one small-cap manager observed,

> Peter Sidoti has built a business of hiring pretty junior kinds of analysts . . . but his business is basically to bring the managements of these companies around to visit with institutions. They hold four or five conferences a year at various locations that provide access to companies. Their focus is exclusively on the small-cap sector, so that's really where most of our assets are focused. And so what we're paying for is to have access to the managements of these companies.[29]

Of course, other firms also provide clients with access to corporate management, but few have been able to compete as effectively as Sidoti in the small- and midcap segments. In describing how he thinks about the firm's business model, Peter Sidoti explained:

> The analogy I run is Southwest Airlines ten years ago. When Southwest got up and running, it ran primarily in the smaller markets. It had a very

low cost structure. It had a young group of people. It didn't fly into La-Guardia and Kennedy, it flew into Islip. It didn't fly into Boston, it flew into Providence. It flew into Love Field in Dallas. It both competed with the big airlines and it didn't. And we're kind of the same way. Nobody really competes with us directly . . . but they all do compete with us. We are all competing for the same commission dollars.[30]

Sidoti typically hires analysts who have worked on Wall Street for only a few years in a noninvestment capacity or who have just graduated from college. It then trains them to function as analysts. Jennifer Scutti, a vice president in the research department, explained:

> We will hire people who have little or no experience in sell-side equity research. They all have strong finance backgrounds; they may have come from other areas on Wall Street; they may have come from industry—all different backgrounds. But the financial skills are there, it's just they don't typically have sell-side experience.[31]

New hires are brought into the research department directly as senior research analysts; the firm does not hire associates or junior analysts. During their first six months, analysts are expected to obtain their relevant licenses and begin covering their first company. Although there is no formal training program, Scutti and other managers work with new analysts to ensure that they are on track to meet their objectives. After the initial six-month introduction, analysts are expected to pick up an additional three companies every six months, until they reach a critical mass of fifteen stocks.

To initiate coverage of a company, analysts publish an eight-page initiation of coverage report including text and models. Stocks are rated as either buy (if expected appreciation for the next twelve months is at least 25 percent) or neutral (if expected appreciation is less than 25 percent). Stocks are not rated as sell.[32] Rating changes, which are accompanied by more detailed reports and updated models, require manager approval.

Sidoti's research is distributed by a thirty-two-person sales force (which targets buy-side firms in the United States, Canada, and Europe) and via electronic platforms such as First Call. Salespeople are industry generalists, divided by region, and are compensated solely on commission. The firm also operates a five-person trading desk that trades all U.S. equities, including companies not covered by its research department. Virtually 98 percent of the firm's revenues are from commissions, 75 percent generated by the trading desk and 25 percent from commission-sharing agreements with larger brokerage firms.[33]

Leerink Swann

Leerink Swann (LS) was founded by Jeff Leerink and six investment banking colleagues in 1995 to provide institutional investors with a unique, high-quality sell-side research product in the health care space.[34] Leerink believed that despite the surplus of Wall Street research available at the time, the health care industry remained poorly served. "Given the several-billion dollar market for research," Leerink argued, "we only need to have a small slice, but we need to make sure we were doing something very different."[35]

To differentiate its research from other firms, Leerink and his long-time friend Dr. Dan Dubin, a research dermatologist at Brigham and Women's Hospital in Boston, established MEDACorp in 1996. A 50–50 joint venture between Leerink and Dubin, MEDACorp created a prescreened network of doctors who provided Leerink's clients with expert insights into medical products, technologies, and services. Dubin served as its president and was responsible for recruiting physicians and managing the network.

Physicians who belong to the MEDACorp network are compensated for the time they spend with Leerink clients. The physicians work as consultants largely on a nonexclusive basis. This model differs from the contingency-fee model employed in many other consulting arrangements and has proved to be a key tool in recruiting for the network. By the end of its first year, 100 physicians had signed up with MEDACorp.

Leerink and his cofounders developed in-house trading capabilities to provide the firm with a mechanism for getting paid for its research product and the advice provided by the MEDACorp physicians. Leerink also felt strongly that the trading desk provided the firm with a valuable information source: "We decided to do the trading ourselves rather than have someone else do it for us and get all that valuable information for themselves."[36]

Leerink hired and trained a sales force to serve as a bridge between the MEDACorp network and the firm's client base, which in the early days consisted largely of hedge funds. As Dubin described it, "We just provided access to professionals with great insights. Early adopters were savvy enough to harness these insights, and convert them to investment decisions."[37]

As LS built out its traditional research product, what emerged was a unique hybrid sell-side research model. The MEDACorp network provides clients with a range of services, including:

- Conference calls with relevant experts, either one-on-one or with other clients, that provide a forum to discuss specific products and ideas;
- Surveys of network participants that provide a variety of expert opinions on a particular topic;
- Conferences and other investor events that provide clients with access to MEDACorp experts;
- In-office visits where MEDACorp professionals visit clients and discuss topics of interest to them.

In some instances, LS offers these services to clients, and in other cases it responds to client requests for services.

To complement the MEDACorp products and services, LS built a sell-side research department. Newly hired research analysts were assigned to cover a set of health care stocks and produce company research reports, earnings estimates, and stock recommendations. In addition to using traditional information resources, LS analysts had access to the MEDACorp network. Dubin observed, "We ended up with an intellectual capital hub that was unique on Wall Street. We had analysts and we had medical experts. They were distinct assets and offered different access points to the information."[38] Clients could use LS's traditional research product, and they could have direct access to the MEDACorp network.

LS is compensated for its research primarily through commissions paid to its trading desk. Clients are not charged directly for time spent with MEDACorp experts or for investment research, but sales force members are responsible for monitoring access to these resources and ensuring that clients funnel sufficient trade volumes through LS's trading desk.

By 2009, LS's MEDACorp network had grown to more than 30,000 members, with many providing consulting services exclusively to MEDA-Corp. The firm's research department included more than twenty investment professionals covering over 150 stocks. And the firm had expanded beyond investment research, establishing an investment banking business, a strategic consulting practice, and launching a health-care-focused private equity fund.

Gerson Lehrman Group

Gerson Lehrman Group (GLG) is an alternative research firm that provides clients with private consultations with industry experts.[39] Founded in 1998, the firm is a pioneer in the expert network segment. By 2012, it had approximately 800 employees and more than 300,000 subject-matter experts located throughout the world. (As of 2008, 70 percent of these experts were located in the United States, 15 percent in Europe, and 10 percent in Asia). Its 2008 revenues were roughly $280 million, and it had an estimated 90 percent share of the expert network market (70 percent, according to Integrity Research).[40]

The core of GLG's business model is matching subject-matter experts, or "council members," with clients seeking their expertise. The company's network of council members is organized vertically into six industry-based sectors (health care; consumer goods and services; real estate; technology, media, and telecommunications; financial and business services; and energy and industrials) and two horizontal groupings (accounting and financial analysis, and legal and regulation). Council members are not GLG employees but consultants who sign a nonexclusive contract to work for the company on a project-by-project basis. They therefore represent "flexible capacity," as they are paid only for hours worked. In 2009, hourly rates, set by the counsel members themselves, ranged from $50 upward with a median of $350, and the typical council member was hired for forty-five minutes per year.

In addition to individual council members, GLG has 300 council partner firms, including Credit Suisse Group and Frost & Sullivan. Employees of these firms are part of the GLG expert network, but their firm rather than the individual receives compensation from GLG for project participation.

GLG council members perform a wide range of projects, including phone consultations, written reports, surveys, market studies, private visits, seminars, and round tables. In 2009, GLG arranged more than 20,000 "transactions" or projects per month, 12,000 of which were phone consultations. While phone consultations are the mainstay of its business, larger and more complex client projects have become increasingly popular.

Council members are recruited via professional publications, career websites, conferences, and travel shows. GLG divides these recruiting efforts into three categories: "name recruiting"—recruiting a specific individual, which is expensive but low risk in that the individual is known; "title recruiting"—recruiting someone with a particular job function, such as VP of marketing; and "population recruiting"—recruiting someone who might have knowledge on a particular topic. Referrals by existing council members are the primary source of new GLG network members.

In 2008, GLG's client base included 850 clients in eighteen countries. The average corporate client paid GLG approximately $250,000 and used the service 150 to 180 times per year. Financial services firms, primarily investment managers, provided 90 percent of its revenues. Michael Blumstein, GLG's former CFO, explained that the growth of the firm's business among investment managers was at least partially attributable to a decline in the value of sell-side research following Reg FD and the Global Settlement, which led buy-side firms to look for other information sources. Other clients included private equity firms, investment banks, law firms, and professional services organizations. Several sell-side firms, such as Credit Suisse and Morgan Stanley (via its AlphaWise division), partner with GLG to provide their own analysts with access to GLG's experts.

The earliest client contracts were fixed-price subscriptions, where clients paid $60,000 for unlimited access to council members in a single sector or $1 million for unlimited access to all sectors for a six-month period. Over the years, this pricing model evolved to incorporate a flexible model, with clients paying a basic access fee and a per usage fee. However, in 2008, fixed rate subscriptions continued to comprise about 70 to 75 percent of the company's revenues.

In discussing the company's business model, Laurence Herman, GLG's general counsel, observed, "We know it is very easy to introduce an expert to a client; the barriers to entry in that sense are incredibly low. The barriers to entry to doing this in an appropriate way, however, are actually quite high."[41] To create competitive advantage, GLG has compiled a database on council members' specific areas of expertise and usage. New council members are asked a series of qualifying questions that allows GLG's employees to better understand their specific knowledge base beyond the broad sector classifications. In addition, GLG ranks council members using data on their usage rates by independent clients. The 5 percent highest-rated council members are labeled "leaders" and the next 20 percent "scholars." This database enables GLG to have confidence that council members who are deployed can answer clients' questions and provide a high-quality consultation.

GLG's service potentially provides its clients with access to private information, an advantage over public sell-side research. But it also carries a risk that experts violate legal and employer restrictions on the disclosure of proprietary information. GLG's compliance policies are designed to manage this risk. For example, council members are precluded from disclosing material nonpublic information about a publicly traded company, from disclosing confidential information, or from giving investment advice. Each year council members sign a contract and complete on-line training to reaffirm these policies; prior to each new project, an e-mail is sent to the relevant council member reviewing the relevant compliance regulations. In addition, employees of publicly traded companies are prohibited from joining the GLG network without their employers' approval.

Conclusions

The research firms discussed in this chapter have pursued strategies to address many of the challenges identified in previous chapters that affect research—high costs of information production and low costs of reproduction, rapid information obsolescence in an efficient capital market, experience good attributes, and information overload.

All have built or are attempting to build reputations among clients for providing valuable investment research: Bernstein for its detailed independent analysis of large-cap stocks; Credit Suisse for its research on large cap stocks that is tailored to client demands; Merrill Lynch for its global view and research tailored to hedge funds; Sidoti for its access to management of micro-, small-, and midcap stocks; Leerink Swann for its access to proprietary information combined with research in the health sector; and Gerson Lehrman Group for its network of experts. Research departments that succeed in building strong reputations help portfolio managers and buy-side analysts to efficiently identify research that is reliable and reduce information overload.

In addition, all the firms are seeking to differentiate the services they provide to their most valuable clients from those provided to lower-valued accounts. Credit Suisse's most valued clients receive access to its full complement of services (research reports, access to corporate management, and so on). Bernstein increasingly monitors whether clients are providing sufficient business to justify the resources they are consuming and is willing to have difficult conversations with those where there was a mismatch. Sidoti provides access to senior executives of small and midcap stocks for its best clients. Leerink Swann's best clients have access to its MEDACorp network and its research. By providing their most valued clients with private access to their analysts, to corporate managers, and to experts these firms reduce research obsolescence and mitigate competitive pressures in the industry.

GLG's consulting business and Leerink Swann's MEDACorp deserve separate discussion. Their research cost structure is quite different from traditional firms. Research costs are incurred each time they organize a consultation for a client and that research is not re-produced or re-distributed. As a result, their business model is not subject to the same pricing pressures faced by traditional research departments. In addition, expert consultations provide clients with private benefits that reduce the problem of research obsolescence faced by traditional sell-side research. Finally, by tracking the ratings of their experts and using that information to better match clients with experts, they are able to increase the value of their service to clients.

Of course, the current success of a firm's research model in delivering value for clients and rents to the provider does not guarantee its long-term sustainability. Sustainability depends on whether existing or new competitors can successfully imitate a particular research model or whether substitute forms of research arise. Imitation is difficult to prevent. Competitors can hire away key individuals or teams that are responsible for a firm's success, and they may be able to eventually replicate key processes. Managers at highly rated research departments may fail to notice competitive threats, particularly for competitors that use new technologies and do not look similar.

However, some resources are difficult to imitate or acquire. Examples include firm reputations, corporate cultures, processes and dynamic capabilities, and network advantages that make it costly for customers or factors to switch to another firm. These types of immobile or imperfectly immobile resources create barriers to entry for competitors. Are there such barriers to entry for the sell-side firms discussed earlier in this chapter? Several firms have already established important barriers. Bernstein has a long-standing reputation for research quality and independence. Its culture and commitment to research enable it to continue to excel in hiring and training star analysts that have proven difficult for other firms to replicate. Leerink Swann and Gerson Lehrman Group have quickly established reputations for providing clients with access to high-quality potentially proprietary information. BofA Merrill Lynch's global reach and scale might be a source of sustainable competitive advantage if the firm continues to find ways to produce timely integrated global and cross-asset class industry research.

Gerson Lehrman Group's network of experts and client list also act as a significant barrier to potential competitors. Because it was the first mover in the industry and quickly managed to build scale, both potential new experts and customers find Gerson Lehrman Group particularly attractive. For new experts, the firm offers a larger base of potential clients, and for clients a broader base of experts. Furthermore, Gerson Lehrman Group's historical ratings of experts by clients enable it to outperform new entrants by leveraging experts who are well suited to match a client's demands.

By focusing on small- and midcap stocks and building relations with corporate managers at these firms, Sidoti hopes to take advantage of a void in this market to support investment firms interested in it, as well as to position itself to participate in IPOs of successful companies in this segment. Given the large number of companies in this segment, further success by Sidoti is likely to invite competition. Sidoti may be able to outperform potential competitors in identifying firms to cover with the greatest investment potential. But it is unclear whether this can provide an effective barrier to entry. The success of the firm's strategy in the long term therefore remains an open question.

The same concerns are relevant for Credit Suisse. If competitors recognize the value of its new approach to measuring analyst and account profitability, there appear to be few (if any) barriers to imitating the measurement system. This does not mean that sell-side research at Credit Suisse will necessarily die, but it does suggest that the current profitability of research may be difficult to sustain.

8

Sell-Side Research in Emerging Markets

Following its exit from investment banking, Prudential announced in 2001 that it planned to double the size of its international securities business over the subsequent three years. The firm targeted Taiwan, Korea, Latin America, and Western Europe as attractive markets for expansion.[1] Prudential was not alone in seeing the promise of sell-side research in emerging markets. Many U.S. and European firms have expanded their operations in developing markets to take advantage of the growth opportunities they present.

In this chapter, we examine the evolution of financial markets and sell-side research in two of the fastest growing emerging markets, China and India. Due to their size, China and India are worthy of study in their own right. In addition, the differences in their evolution make them interesting markets to examine.

Development of Financial Markets in China and India

Several factors limit stock market development in emerging countries. First, in the early stages of their economic development, emerging economies frequently place restrictions on the purchase of domestic shares by foreign investors. Second, for many companies, most of the shares outstanding are owned by the government or by founding families, restricting liquidity. Third, domestic institutional investors are typically under-developed and play little role in capital markets. Finally, institutions that facilitate trust in financial markets, such as auditors, research analysts, in-vestment banks, and regulators, are typically underdeveloped. These fac-tors have influenced the development of local Chinese and Indian stock markets and sell-side research.

China

Chinese households have among the highest savings rates in the world, conserving 28 percent of disposable income in 2008.[2] However, house-hold investment options are tightly controlled. Households earn low reg-ulated returns on savings deposits in state-owned banks. They can invest in real property, or they can invest in the local stock market, where the government continues to be the largest shareholder.

At the inception of its domestic stock markets, China created A- and B-class shares that were listed on the Shanghai and Shenzhen markets. A shares could be purchased only by local investors, whereas B shares were available only to individual foreign investors. Although denominated in local Chinese currency, B shares could be bought and sold in foreign currency. Any dividends were declared in Chinese currency but paid in foreign currency and could be sent abroad freely despite China's strict ex-change controls. In addition, certain Chinese companies were permitted to list on the Hong Kong stock exchange as H shares that were available to foreign retail and institutional investors.

This structure effectively created a two-tiered market. Domestic retail investors own A shares listed on the Shanghai and Shenzhen exchanges. Retail trading volume is estimated to account for between 67 percent[3] and 90 percent[4] of total trading volume on these markets, and individual investors account for 99 percent of the 150 million trading accounts.[5] The retail influence has produced markets with high turnover and high vola-tility. According to Terence Ho, a specialist in the Chinese market with Ernst & Young, "All the shares of companies listed in Shanghai change hands about once every four or five months. That's too often—it's specu-lative. On the other hand, if markets are too dominated by intuitional investors, you have stable share prices but less liquidity."[6]

The B shares created for foreign retail investors have traded at a sizable discount to A shares and have low liquidity. China has changed its laws to allow international investors to purchase domestic shares. The Quali-fied Foreign Investor Program (December 2002) permits foreign inves-tors to trade up to $30 billion of A shares. But, as a research director of one global bank explained, international investment in China's domestic market

> accounts for only about 1 percent of the volume—the remaining 99 per-cent is from domestic investors. This is an extremely regulated market and in many ways the Chinese government is quite protectionist in the way that it operates the market. There is limited access for foreign broker-age firms because they only license Chinese nationals, which has slowed the development of the market.

Global investors interested in China have focused more on the Hong Kong market. The head of Asian research for a U.S. firm observed that this has had an impact on sell-side research, noting that "increasingly, in-stitutional money is finding its way into Asia through the Hong Kong ex-change, which tracks the volume of trading being done by international institutional investors . . . and it's those entities that are looking for more long-term fundamental research."

By mid-2011, 592 Chinese companies had listed on the Hong Kong Exchange, compared to 917 on the Shanghai Exchange.[7] Chinese list-ings comprised 58 percent of the market capitalization of the Hong Kong Exchange and 66 percent of its total trading volume. In addition, in mid-2011, sixty-seven Chinese companies were listed on the NYSE and 127 on NASDAQ.[8] For the period from 2001 to 2010, the index return for China's Shanghai Exchange was 35.4 percent, compared to 681.5 percent for the Hong Kong Hang Seng China Composite (see Exhibit 8.1). Ana-lysts and money managers we interviewed explained that the strong per-formance of the Hong Kong market relative to the Shanghai reflects the higher proportion of poorly performing state-owned Chinese enterprises listed on the Shanghai exchange and the impact of retail investing. In con-trast, the Hong Kong market covers many of the dynamic entrepreneurial (non–state-owned) companies in China and is more institutionally based.

Research on Chinese companies is affected by the unreliability of re-ported information on Chinese companies' performance. In 2011, IMD World Competitiveness ranked China fifty-second (out of fifty-nine) in auditing and accounting quality. Weak disclosure and governance, one analyst observed, leads analysts to focus on such topics as

Exhibit 8.1   Performance of major developed and developing stock markets.

Country	Number of equity IPOs from Jan. 2006 to Mar. 2011	Index return 2001–2010 (percentage)	Index return 2001–2006 (percentage)
China			
Shanghai Exchange	1,089	35.4%	29.0%
Hang Seng China		681.5	536.7
India			
Sensex	308	416.3	247.1
Japan			
Nikkei 225	405	−25.8	25.0
FTSE 100	247	−5.2	−0.03
United States			
S&P 500	1011	−4.7	7.4

SOURCE: Capital IQ (Number of IPOs for companies headquartered in each country, excludes closed end funds and REITs) and Datastream.

management's background, cross-holdings between families and companies, and the underlying politics. Who is perhaps going to sell their shareholding? Who might want to acquire someone else's shareholding? . . . By and large information availability is a lot less than in the U.S. and that's why I think analysts probably still add more value in the investment process here than they do in developed markets.

In addition, given the low ratings of China's freedom of the press, where the country received a score of eighty-four versus an average of nineteen for the United States, the United Kingdom, and Japan, investors cannot rely on independent media scrutiny of listed companies.[9] One analyst estimated that 80 to 85 percent of the market value of the Chinese stock market is comprised of companies that are government regulated or government owned, and fifteen of the top twenty stocks (by market capitalization) are state-owned enterprises (SOEs). Given government control of the media and commitment to support key firms, as well as evolving enforcement and governance, the information environment for international investors is opaque.

Information opacity and government regulation make the task of analyzing Chinese stocks particularly challenging. One Chinese investment analyst explained that, when you buy a stock in China:

You're buying a company which doesn't know its sales volume, its sales price, its raw material cost, and cannot plan anything ahead more than two or three months. So you're not buying entrepreneurs and you're not buying management, you're not buying management strategy. You're making a bet on the country and the government more than picking a stock.

Another analyst demonstrated the impact of government regulation on investment performance using the case of China Mobile, the largest mobile operator in China:

> From 2000 onwards, investments in China Mobile would have done well in the market and in absolute terms too. You didn't have to think too much about it. And that was simply because China Mobile was the one company with a GSM license. Two other firms were granted mobile licenses for different technologies that could not compete with GSM. The government had effectively given China Mobile a free run until 2007. So if you understood that this is a company which is backed by government policy with the right technology and the right licenses, all you had to do was buy it because you're going from 100 million phone users to 600 million phone users over the next seven, eight years. . . . But in 2007, the government suddenly decided that it was not right to have one company with a market share of about 85 to 90% and we need more competition. So they changed the rules. They gave out new licenses and restructured the industry. Since that policy change, China Mobile's stock has collapsed and has substantially underperformed the market. So if you got that policy right up and down, you were fine. But none of these decisions were made by China Mobile's management or reflected its strategy. The company did not have any real leeway in what they were trying to do. Their success was because of something given to them by the government and the underperformance was because of something that was taken away by the government.

Ding Yuan, a professor of accounting at the China Europe International Business School, explained that, as a result of the challenges discussed in the preceding paragraphs, "The majority of investors in China, including fund managers, don't really pay attention to the fundamentals. Instead, there's a lot of trading and buying based on privileged information, bordering on insider trading."[10]

India

The story in India is somewhat different. Like China, Indian households have high savings rates, conserving 32 percent of disposable income in 2008.[11] However, Indian household savings are more likely to be invested in physical assets, such as land, gold, and silver, rather than financial assets.[12]

The percentage of Indian household savings invested in financial assets, and specifically in stocks and bonds, has actually declined in recent years. According to the Securities and Exchange Board of India, "Investment in shares and debentures by the households as a proportion of financial savings decreased significantly from 12.4 percent in 2007–08 to 2.6 percent in 2008–09."[13] Individual investors are estimated to hold approximately 16 percent of the equity of publicly traded companies in India.[14]

Like China, India also initially restricted foreign individuals and institutions from buying or selling Indian stocks. However, in 1991, the Indian government relaxed these restrictions and permitted foreign institutions to purchase Indian stocks. Exhibit 8.2 shows that annual foreign investment in Indian stocks rose rapidly thereafter. In the fiscal year 2009–2010, net portfolio investments in India by foreign institutional investors totaled $32 billion, up from a net outflow of $13.9 billion over the previous twelve-month period.[15]

Exhibit 8.2 Foreign investment flows into India.

Year	Direct Investment US$ in millions	Portfolio Investment US$ in millions	Total US$ in millions
1990–1991	$97	$6	$103
1991–1992	$129	$4	$133
1992–1993	$315	$244	$559
1993–1994	$586	$3,567	$4,153
1994–1995	$1,314	$3,824	$5,138
1995–1996*	$2,144	$2,748	$4,892
1996–1997*	$2,821	$3,312	$6,133
1997–1998*	$3,557	$1,828	$5,385
1998–1999*	$2,462	–$61	$2,401
1999–2000*	$2,155	$3,026	$5,181
2000–2001*	$4,029	$2,760	$6,789
2001–2002*	$6,130	$2,021	$8,151
2002–2003*	$5,035	$979	$6,014
2003–2004*	$4,322	$11,377	$15,699
2004–2005*	$6,051	$9,315	$15,366
2005–2006*	$8,961	$12,492	$21,453
2006–2007*	$22,826	$7,003	$29,829
2007–2008*	$34,835	$27,271	$62,106
2008–2009*	$37,838	–$13,855	$23,983
2009–2010*P	$37,763	$32,376	$70,139
2010–2011*P	$30,380	$31,471	$61,851

P = Provisional. Note: (1) Data for 2009–2010, 2010–2011 and April 2011–December 2011 are provisional. (2) Data from 1995–1996 onward include acquisition of shares of Indian companies by nonresidents under Section 6 of FEMA, 1999. Data on such acquisitions are included as part of FDI since January 1996. (3) Data on FDI have been revised since 2000–2001 with expanded coverage to approach international best practices. Data from 2000–2001 onward are not comparable with FDI data for earlier years. (4) Negative (–) sign indicates outflow. (5) Direct Investment data for 2006–2007 include swap of shares of 3.1 billion.
SOURCE: RBI, SEBI, www.sebi.gov.in/cms/sebi_data/attachdocs/1340250093262.pdf; retrieved in September 2012.

Finally, due to its British Empire legacy, India has more developed capital market institutions than China. India ranked thirty-third out of fifty-nine in the 2011 IMD World Competitiveness rankings on auditing and accounting quality, and in 2011 India's Freedom House media rating was thirty-three.[16] These ratings were not materially different from those of developed countries such as the United Kingdom, the United States, and Japan, implying that the quality of company information available to investors from financial reports and the Indian media is comparable to that found in developed economies.

These factors have combined to generate impressive returns for Indian stocks. For the period 2001 to 2010, the return for the Indian Sensex Index was 416.3 percent, compared to −25.8 percent for Japan's Nikkei 225, −5.2 percent for the U.K. FTSE 100, and −4.7 percent for the U.S. S&P 500 (look again at Exhibit 8.1). The poor performance of developed market indices cannot be attributed to the financial crisis of 2007–2008, as index returns for 2001–2006, prior to the crisis, tell a similar story.

Growth in Sell-Side Research in China and India

The development of financial markets in China and India has been accompanied by an increase in sell-side research. Exhibit 8.3 compares the number of senior sell-side analysts in China and India for the period 1982 to

Exhibit 8.3   Sell-side analysts by country.

	1982	1989	1997	2004	2011
Global	2,022	5,044	12,058	14,934	20,312
High-growth emerging markets					
China	0	64	376	594	850
India	0	0	116	137	1,087
Subtotal	0	64	492	731	1,937
Percentage of global market	0%	1%	4%	5%	10%
Established markets					
Japan	0	261	507	478	695
United Kingdom	0	1,131	1,795	2,603	2,549
United States	1,915	3,021	5,834	5,595	5,878
Subtotal	1,915	4.413	8,136	8,676	9,122
Percentage of global market	95%	87%	67%	58%	45%

SOURCE: Nelson.

2011 with those for three of the leading developed countries—the United States, the United Kingdom, and Japan. Early in this period sell-side research was almost exclusively located in the United States. Indeed, the United States continues to be the largest sell-side research market and has tripled in size since 1982. However, the number of senior U.S. analysts has remained relatively stable since 1997. Other developed markets, such as the United Kingdom and Japan, experienced impressive growth in sell-side research between 1982 and 2004. But there, too, growth has flattened. In contrast, China and India had only a few sell-side analysts until the 1990s; the number of analysts in both countries has since grown dramatically. By 2011, these two emerging markets accounted for 10 percent of the global sell-side industry versus 4 percent in 1997 and 5 percent in 2004.

The rapid growth of equity research in China and India is reflected in analyst coverage among the largest companies. Exhibit 8.4 shows coverage from 2001 to 2011 for U.S., Chinese, and Indian companies listed on the Dow Jones Industrial Average, Hang Seng China Composite, and Sensex indices, which represent some of their leading listed companies. Average coverage for Chinese listed stocks grew from twelve analysts to twenty-seven during this period. In 2001, coverage of Chinese companies was roughly 70 percent of leading U.S. companies; by 2011 it had increased to around 90 percent.

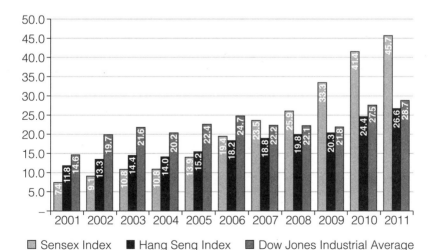

Exhibit 8.4. Average number of analysts covering component stocks, 2001–2011.
SOURCE: Bloomberg.

Coverage of Indian stocks rose even more sharply, from seven analysts to almost forty-six. (See Exhibit 8.5 for recent data on coverage for leading stocks on the Indian market.) To put this growth in perspective, coverage of the leading Indian company was 50 percent lower than that for leading U.S. firms in 2001; by 2011, it was almost 60 percent higher. Indeed, one money manager observed, "The market has become crowded . . . given the number of people covering stocks."

The growing scale and liquidity of Chinese and Indian companies has contributed to the economic viability of sell-side research. In explaining the growth of sell-side research in India, one money manager observed:

> The trajectory of the number of companies that ought to be covered goes up year after year mainly on account of 8% GDP growth and around 15% growth in the corporate sector. . . . Around 700 companies are currently traded fairly well. However, if you just go back four or five years . . . only 300 companies had sufficient volume to support research. . . . Between 2010 and 2020, [growth] for the corporate sector is expected to be around 11%. . . . With that kind of growth, more and more companies every year become eligible to be covered by analysts.

Consistent with this observation, from 2005 to 2010, the number of companies with a market capitalization of $500 million or greater increased by 846 percent on Chinese exchanges and by 186 percent on the Mumbai exchanges.[17] (See Exhibit 8.6.)

The scale of Chinese and Indian IPOs stocks has also supported the increase in sell-side research. As shown in Exhibit 8.1, from January 2006 to March 2011 the Chinese market had more IPOs than the United States, and India had more than the United Kingdom. In 2010 alone, 490 Chinese companies had IPOs valued at $102 billion. Of these, 347 (valued at $72 billion) were on the Shanghai and Shenzhen exchanges, and eighty-two (worth $35 billion) were in Hong Kong. The Agricultural Bank of China was the largest IPO in 2010 at $22 billion, with shares offered on both the Shanghai and Hong Kong exchanges. The year 2010 was also a strong one for Indian IPOs, with sixty-three new listings raising $8.3 billion (up from twenty and $4.1 billion in 2009). During the same year, the United States had 154 IPOs that raised $38.7 billion, and the United Kingdom had fifty offerings worth $10.1 billion.[18]

Not surprisingly, given the greater access of global institutional investors to the Indian market, global banks have played a more prominent role in Indian IPO markets than in China. Exhibit 8.7 shows the league

Exhibit 8.5 Number of analysts covering BSE stocks historically.

Company name	2001	2002	2003	2004	2005	2006	2007	2008	2009	2010	2011
Acc Ltd	9	12	10	12	13	23	29	31	38	46	
Ambuja Cements	10	10	10	11	16	24	25	29			
Bajaj Auto Ltd											56
Bajaj Holding SA	7	10	14	13	15	22	23				
Bharat Heavy Ele	6	5	8	12	14	15	19	25	35	45	46
Bharti Airtel				12	13	18	26	27	35	48	53
Castrol India	3	5	7								
Cipla Ltd	8	12	11	11	13	21	22	23			41
Colgate Palmoliv		6	7								
DLF Ltd								22	31	38	39
Dr Reddy's Labs	9	13	14	14	18	19	27				
GlaxoSmithKline	8	9	11								
Grasim Inds Ltd	12	10	12	11	11	19	23	26	35	38	
HCL Tech Ltd		12	9								
HDFC Bank Ltd				9	15	20	30	32	43	48	50
Hero Honda Motor		9	11	12	16	20	23			52	52
Hindalco Inds	5	8	9	9	9	17	18	24	26	36	37
Hindustan Petro	3	10	13	11	18						
Hindustan Unilev	11	10	16	13	14	19	22	22	31	41	45
Housing Dev Fin			9	9	9	12	17	21	28	31	39
Icici Bank Ltd			11	8	15	21	27	34	37	42	53
Icici Ltd	11	11									
Infosys Tech Ltd	12	16	10	15	15	26	35	33	47	53	65
ITC Ltd	10	9	12	11	11	16	18	24	29	39	45
Jaiprakash Assoc								16	17	21	28
Jindal Steel & P											22
Larsen & Toubro	10	10	8	9	14	17	19	22	32	39	40
Mahanagar Tele	8	7	12	7							
Mahindra & Mahin	7							25	32	40	45
Maruti Suzuki In					17	21	25	31	38	51	59
Nestle India Ltd	9	6	9								
Niit Ltd	5										
NTPC Ltd						17	16	21	36	45	46
Oil & Natural Ga				11	19	20	22	29	30	38	48
Ranbaxy Labs Ltd	8	12	16	10	19	20	26	23	30		
Reliance Communi							15	27	35	41	44
Reliance Inds	6	8	10	12	14	16	22	25	31	38	43
Reliance Infrast	1	3	6	7	4	12	10	14	22	23	24
Reliance Petrole	0	0									
Satyam Computer	12	13	12	13	16	23	30	31			
State Bank Ind	6	7	13	11	13	21	29	30	41	46	50
Sterlite Industr									26	36	42
Sun Pharma Indu									32	42	
Tata Consultancy						23	30	31	43	48	60
Tata Motors Ltd	7	11	14	13	16	24	26	29	31	44	48
Tata Power Co				6	9	14			29	38	35
Tata Steel Ltd	3	9	9	12	11	18	19	26	34	45	49
Wipro Ltd				15	18	24	33	27	45	49	58
Zee Entertainmen	7	9	11	6	12						

NOTE: Blank cells indicate that the company was not part of the Sensex during that year.
SOURCE: Data compiled by Hitesh Zaveri, 2011.

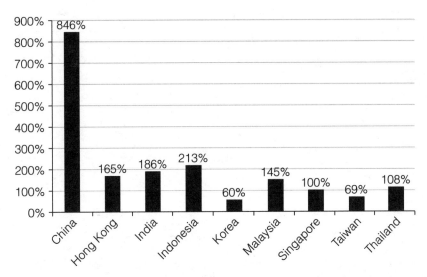

Exhibit 8.6. Increase in the number of US$500 million stocks (percentage change, 2005–2010).
SOURCE: Credit Suisse, "Research Strategic Initiatives," February 2011.

tables for Chinese and Indian IPOs from 2000 to 2010. For the top fifteen underwriters in each market, domestic Indian banks had a 14 percent market share, versus 35 percent for domestic Chinese banks. In India, the leading domestic firms, Kotak Mahindra Capital and ICICI Securities, ranked third and fourth respectively, whereas in China, domestic firms took all top four positions (China International Capital, CITIC, China Galaxy Securities, and Bank of China).

Finally, the scale of domestic demand for goods and services in India and China makes their markets important for global companies, generating additional coverage for the region by sell-side analysts. As one Asian analyst explained:

> The supply chain is becoming internationalized. You can't talk about the luxury goods companies in Europe without talking about what is going on in Asia. Increasingly, their business, especially their growth, is being driven by what's occurring in the Asia-Pacific region . . . 5 percent, 10 percent, 15 percent of their business is coming out of China and India. . . . I was in the United States just before Christmas talking with one of our consumer analysts who just spent a week on the ground in China and India visiting companies, and getting a sense of local positioning versus that of multinationals. And to her that was the biggest differentiator in

Exhibit 8.7   Equity IPO League tables for India and China from 2000 to 2010.

	Book runner	Proceeds (US$ million)	Market share	Number of issues
Panel A: China				
1	China International Capital Co.	97,427.25	12.4	99
2	CITIC Securities Co. Ltd.	59,447.91	7.6	122
3	China Galaxy Securities Co.	26,463.87	3.4	39
4	BOC International (China) Ltd.	24,474.27	3.1	54
5	Morgan Stanley (Asia) Ltd.	23,815.91	3.0	75
6	Guotai Junan Securities	22,751.85	2.9	59
7	UBS Investment Bank	22,552.47	2.9	87
8	Goldman Sachs (Asia)	21,545.15	2.7	66
9	UBS Securities Co. Ltd.	18,957.22	2.4	27
10	Guosen Securities Co. Ltd.	14,606.52	1.9	123
11	Haitong Securities Co. Ltd.	12,925.16	1.6	55
12	Credit Suisse	12,709.59	1.6	73
13	Pingan Securities Co. Ltd.	12,654.14	1.6	115
14	Deutsche Bank Asia	12,473.02	1.6	38
15	Merrill Lynch International (Asia)	12,120.28	1.5	24
Panel B: India				
1	Citi	14,902.09	6.3	85
2	DSP Merrill Lynch Ltd.	8,856.55	3.7	84
3	Kotak Mahindra Capital Co.	8,712.72	3.7	101
4	ICICI Securities & Finance Co.	8,687.68	3.7	131
5	UBS Investment Bank	7,388.81	3.1	51
6	Enam Securities	6,314.01	2.7	80
7	Deutsche Bank Asia	6,203.16	2.6	45
8	SBI Capital Markets Ltd.	5,526.84	2.3	118
9	Morgan Stanley	5,326.73	2.2	30
10	JM Morgan Stanley	5,050.30	2.1	66
11	JP Morgan Secs (Asia) (HK)	4,412.54	1.9	31
12	Citigroup	4,210.26	1.8	37
13	JP Morgan	4,142.32	1.7	21
14	Merrill Lynch	4,132.45	1.7	20
15	JM Financial Group	4,000.16	1.7	37

SOURCE: ThomsonOne.

terms of what she could go back and write about, and talk to clients about because she lived and breathed it.

Quality of Chinese and Indian Analysts

Despite recent growth, the sell-side industry in Asia remains less mature than that in the United States. One analyst described traditional sell-side research in Asia as "tabloid-type research" with analysts more likely to "report stories rather than analyze companies."

Yet the training of analysts (and hence the quality of their research product) has improved. A buy-side investor in India observed that today

> many analysts have done a post-graduate program in accounting, which is a CPA equivalent, in addition to a bachelor's degree. More than 75% would have an MBA, although probably not from the best schools . . . In addition, if you go to the Chartered Financial Analyst (CFA) examination center in Bombay, it resembles a football game in terms of the number of people applying for the exam. I suspect that we will have more candidates appearing for the exam than anywhere else in the world.

Another buy-side manager observed that improvements in the quality of sell-side research in the Indian market have been driven by the growing presence of international investors: "As a lot of foreign investors came to India towards the late 1990s, the demand for more in-depth research took hold and a lot of quality started appearing. . . . Over this period, we saw a lot of analysts actually doing much more in-depth modeling." He added that a more rigorous process has also arisen around the changing of an investment opinion by an analyst.

However, there continues to be room for improvement. A manager at a leading investment firm opined that there are still only "two analysts per sector who I would talk to. In Hong Kong—and even more so in China—there is an opportunity to improve the style and quality of analysis." Buy-side investors observed that "most sell-side analysts still focus more on short term trading opportunities." Some argued that this short-term investment horizon is the result of the high level of government involvement discussed earlier. One Asian research director explained:

> When you have the likes of China and India where the government plays a significant presence in the economy, whether that's through state-owned or state-run entities, or through a heavier regulatory influence such as for utilities, oil, and financials across the board, it's really difficult from a sell-side analyst's perspective to establish three- to five-year trends, because the regulatory environment and/or the government's thinking about how an industry should develop within their own country can change.

Research Funding in China and India

Many of the key institutional arrangements used to support research in Hong Kong and Mumbai mirror those used in the United States. For example, trading commissions are an important source of funding for Chinese and Indian sell-side research departments. Commission rates in India and Hong Kong are somewhat higher than rates in the United States and Western Europe: ten to fifteen basis points (bps) of trade value in Hong Kong and in India. These are down from forty bps ten years ago,[19] indicating that emerging markets are subject to the same pricing pressures as developed economies. (See Exhibit 8.8 for recent commission and broker revenue in India.) However, in contrast to the United States, total commission revenues in both countries have continued to increase over time as

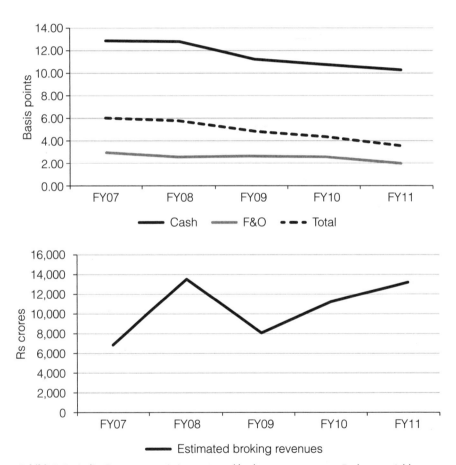

Exhibit 8.8. India: Recent commission rates and brokerage revenues. a. Brokerage yields (*Note*: Cash refers to cash equities and F&O to futures and options transactions.) b. Estimated industry brokerage revenue (*Note*: Amounts in Rs thousands of Crores.)

SOURCE: Karthik Srinivasan and Vibha Batra, "Equity Brokerage Industry," ICRA Ltd., July 2011, p. 4.

increases in the number of shares traded, the number of companies listed, and the value of listed stocks have more than offset declining commission rates. According to Greenwich Associates, Asian equity markets generated $3.8 billion in commissions in 2010, up from $3.3 billion in 2009.[20] In China, commissions on A shares and B shares are no more than thirty bps.[21]

The process used by Indian portfolio managers to allocate commissions to sell-side firms, via a broker voting system, is also similar to that used in the United States. The specific process used varies from firm to firm, but one chief investment officer (CIO) of an Indian buy-side firm explained that the fund managers and analysts at his firm vote to allocate business among brokers on a quarterly basis, with research being considered an important factor in the voting.

A 2009 study by Greenwich Associates indicates that research is an important contributor to the broker votes. The study finds that on average, 66 percent of the allocation of brokerage commissions by Asian buy-side managers was related to assessments of research, sales coverage, and advisory services (compared to 26 percent for trading coverage and agency execution). Key elements of research valued by Asian buy-side clients, as reported by *Institutional Investor*, include integrity, industry knowledge, local country knowledge, and access, similar to those elements valued by U.S. clients.[22]

Sell-side firms allocate a share of the commissions received from clients to the research department. One research department manager at an Asian sell-side firm explained that at his firm the research department receives 30 to 50 percent of commissions earned on delta one products (*delta one* is the term used to describe financial derivatives that have no optionality and includes forwards, swaps, and the like), 30 to 45 percent of cash equities commissions, and 15 to 20 percent of prime brokerage fees. The investment banking division also contributes a portion of the research budget, and a small percentage of commissions earned on electronic trading goes to research.

Finally, in appraising the performance of sell-side analysts, Hong Kong and Mumbai firms again tend to follow U.S. practices, with some country-specific adjustments. For example, sell-side analysts receive regular performance feedback from clients in the form of summaries of client votes, as well as annual surveys by *Institutional Investor* and Thomson Reuters's Extel that rank analysts by industry. One research department manager stated that, even in Asia, "*II* is still the most visible external measure of what people think about individual [analysts]." Compensation levels for sell-side analysts are lower in absolute terms than in the United States but have not fallen materially in recent years. In India, for example, an experienced analyst with a global investment bank might earn a base salary of $300,000 with a bonus of $300,000 to $700,000. At a domestic bank, compensation tends to be lower, around $300,000 all included. Additionally, at least in some Asian markets, sell-side analysts are considerably better compensated than their buy-side counterparts. At many firms, analysts in hot IPO markets get paid significantly more than analysts covering other sectors.

Conclusions

In contrast to the experiences of the United States, where sell-side research is seen as a mature or even declining industry, the sell-side industry has thrived in emerging economies such as China and India. In China, the development of capital markets has lagged behind that of the overall economy due to weak governance, the government's role as the major shareholder in many companies, and continued restrictions on investing in local Chinese companies. As a result, the Shanghai and Shenzhen markets are primarily retail markets that have experienced a boom and subsequent decline in the last decade. In contrast, the less-regulated Hong Kong market, which also lists many Chinese companies, has thrived and contains a greater share of entrepreneurial companies.

The Mumbai stock market is more mature than those of Shanghai and Shenzhen. India has had more experience with the types of institutions and talent required for a successful capital market, including auditors, investment banking, brokers, and a free press. In addition, deregulation in India has permitted institutional investors to invest in Indian companies, a sharp contrast to China.

Despite their differences, both countries have experienced rapid growth in sell-side research, driven by the scale and increased liquidity of the two markets and by the number of IPOs. Coverage of large stocks in both markets has approached or even exceeded that for U.S. stocks. However, there continue to be questions about the quality of research.

The mid- to long-term prospects for stock markets appear to be stronger for China and India than for the United States or Western Europe. Their product markets are expected to continue to grow at robust rates with above-average economic growth, fueling further financial market growth and IPOs and continuing to attract institutional investors in India and Hong Kong. In addition, Chinese leaders appear to recognize the need for easing of currency and investment regulations that have delayed global institutional interest in its domestic stock markets.

All of this is likely to be good news for sell-side research. Business opportunities for new companies generate demand for financing, leading to further IPOs and increased demand for equity research. Increases in the public float of companies in these growing markets generate liquidity and institutional demand, further driving demand for sell-side research. It is estimated that only 19 percent of China's market capitalization is freely floated, versus 31 percent in India. In contrast, the free float is 90 percent in the United States and 61 percent globally.[23]

Of course, the attractive growth opportunities for China and India do not eliminate the prospect of punctuated market contractions. For example, in China the Shanghai Stock Exchange Index grew by almost 390 percent from January 2006 to October 2007 but had fallen by roughly 70 percent one year later. Such volatility is likely to persist in these markets, particularly as concerns grow about inflated Chinese property markets and inflated Indian stock values. Yet their sustained strong economic growth, fueled by growing domestic demand and exports, is expected to persist for many years.

9

Conclusions

Since its inception, the sell-side research industry has shown remarkable resilience given the many challenges it has faced. Its business model has evolved to mitigate problems associated with supplying information goods, such as the challenge in recovering research costs given their low cost of reproduction and rapid obsolescence. It has responded to new regulations, such as the May Day deregulation of commissions, Reg FD, and the Global Settlement, which have challenged its business models. And it has reacted to changes in technology and globalization, which pose both threats and opportunities for the existing players in the industry. Its continued vitality is a testament to the value and importance of financial information to the efficient functioning of our capital markets.

Yet from our study valuable lessons emerge for the industry, for firms in the industry, and for analysts themselves.

Implications for the Industry

Our research indicates that two factors underlie the continued resilience of the sell-side research industry. First, there is a fundamental demand for sell-side information from buy-side institutional investors. It would be economically burdensome for each of the thousands of such institutions to replicate the fundamental research that occurs on the sell side. As a result, buy-side firms are willing to pay for sell-side research, sometimes handsomely. Second, perhaps because it has had to be nimble in responding to the ups and downs of the market itself, the sell-side industry has developed capabilities that have enabled it to adjust its business model as required. When commissions were deregulated, it developed an alternative model that was based on providing investors with the information needed to support new stock offerings as well as secondhand trading. When the research/investment banking market became regulated, financial institutions recognized opportunities to use technology and field research to provide clients with superior proprietary information and to ride the wave of capital market globalization.

In addition, sell-side firms have developed a remarkable capability for managing research effectively. The process of hiring, training, mentoring, and rewarding analysts is sophisticated and supported by highly visible metrics of analyst performance, the industry ratings. Together, these factors have produced an industry that supports the creation and development of human capital required for analysis and the distribution of new ideas, yet is brutally competitive, forcing ineffective analysts to exit. The balance of these forces has served the industry well.

Implications for Regulators

As discussed in this book, regulatory actions in the United States and the United Kingdom have focused on concerns about conflicts of interest faced by sell-side analysts. Analysts face fundamental conflicts between managers of the firms they cover and the investors who acquire their advice. They face pressure to issue optimistic research to increase the odds of generating investment banking and advisory services from corporate managers, to preserve access to management, and to stimulate trading or investment in their banks' IPOs, at the expense of their buy-side clients.

Problems of conflict of interest also apply to the rapidly developing Chinese and Indian sell-side industries discussed in Chapter 8. One portfolio manager observed:

> I've never seen an "underperform" on any of the four large state-owned banks within China. These are government-run and government-owned entities where the government owns two-thirds of them. Putting an "underperform" on them would be telling the market that you have no confidence

in the government and in the banking system itself. If you want to win investment banking mandates, I don't think that it would be a very good business model to put underperforms on there. People certainly recognize that from the buy-side community. They take it with a grain of salt. You know, you understand that you have to read between the lines and often a "market perform" from a certain analyst may actually imply underperform. As long as investment banking is growing and one of the main drivers of sell-side research, I don't see that changing any time in the near future.

These types of conflicts are inherent in the sell-side business and have led to new regulations in the United States designed to mitigate such behavior. However, as long as funding for research is indirect, coming from commission or investment banking revenues, such conflicts of interest will persist. The Global Settlement succeeded in reducing one form of conflict by limiting the connection between banking and research. But it also had the effect of reducing funds available to support sell-side research and failed to address other conflicts faced by analysts, notably analysts' incentives to issue reports that drive trading and hence brokerage revenues. Whether the Global Settlement's support for independent firms offset these effects or is sustainable remains unclear.

The other major U.S. regulation, Regulation Fair Disclosure, designed to level the playing field for retail investors by prohibiting corporate managers from providing privileged information to favored sell-side analysts, also raises important questions about the effectiveness of the U.S. regulations. Sell-side analysts continue to organize conferences that bring together corporate managers and important buy-side clients for small group or one-on-one meetings. The two sides argue that such meetings provide investment context but no new information. However, such context is rated one of the most valued services provided by the sell side. Even if such meetings were banned, given the resources available to large banks and institutional investors, is it realistic to expect that retail and institutional investors will play on a level field?

We suggest that the most effective controls for conflict of interest may come from investment banks themselves. As intermediaries, their own reputations and long-term value depend on their analysts balancing the potentially competing interests of buy-side clients and corporate issuers. If their analysts' reports oversell corporate issuers to buy-side clients, those clients will be unwilling to support future new issues, undermining the sustainability of the bank's underwriting business. Our evidence suggests that, prior to the Global Settlement, analysts at the world's leading investment banks were generally effective in balancing their responsibilities to buy-side clients and corporate issuers. These analysts produced more accurate earnings estimates and more profitable recommendations than their peers at either lower-rated banks or brokerage firms. By caring about their own reputations (and those of their firms), they were able to manage the inherent conflicts of interest.

However, transparency is needed to ensure that bank reputations are effective in limiting research conflicts of interest. Buy-side clients are entitled to know the nature and extent of a bank's affiliations with a company whose stock its analyst recommends. They are entitled to know the track record of an analyst's recommendations and earnings estimates for all stocks covered, the analyst's history of issuing buy recommendations, and the analyst's experience in covering the company in question. We believe that, ultimately, regulation is likely to be most effective if it focuses on ensuring such transparency, allowing investors to make their own minds up about whose research they can trust.

Implications for Sell-Side Firms
Managing Reputational Risk

As the preceding discussion indicates, leading investment banks' reputations depend on preserving a balance between serving the interests of buy-side clients and corporate clients. Similarly, brokerage firms' reputations rely on balancing the short-term and long-term interests of the firm. Research reports that encourage short-term trading but do not create value for clients are likely to undermine the firm's reputation and long-term sustainability. Conflicts of interest, therefore, continue to be ever present in the industry.

The reputational risks posed by conflicts of interest between analysts and different clients were exacerbated by the recent growth of proprietary trading models at banks. Under these models, banks are not merely trading on behalf of their clients but are managing their own portfolios. It is all too tempting for banks to take advantage of inside information, proprietary research, and client trading to profit at the expense of their clients.

To successfully balance these conflicts, research directors need to understand how their analysts add value for different clients (for example, corporate issuers and buy-side clients) and how to manage the firm's reputational risk given conflicts. Reputational risk can be managed by ensuring that (1) employees are regularly trained to understand the firm's value proposition and the risks arising from its status as an intermediary, and then practice managing those risks; (2) the firm maintains internal transparency about the standards of integrity expected from employees and the consequences of failing to meet those standards—for example, analysts' independence is supported throughout the organization; (3) the firm maintains external transparency about its business relationships with clients, as well as its internal standards to protect clients; and (4) the firm has adequate internal controls in place to monitor and enforce these standards. Overall, the most sustainable source of competitive advantage is the firm's culture that supports the four steps firms can use to manage reputational risks.

Questions about research independence and quality in the United States have typically arisen when sell-side analysts (and other firm employees) have focused myopically on meeting short-term company profit goals and individual bonus awards at the expense of long-term reputational risks to the firm. What is most concerning is that there is no way for the firm to claw back the sizable rewards paid to employees in question, even though they came at the expense of shareholders and customers. One creative suggestion for combating this short-term focus was made by the Squam Lake Working Group on Financial Regulation. This group, an independent think tank of respected finance academics, recommended that financial firms hold back payment of a portion of individual bonus awards each year and invest them in treasury bills. As the treasury bills mature, the proceeds would be paid out to employees, provided it is clear that their short-term performance was not at the expense of the firm's reputation. If this condition is not satisfied, the firm could use the proceeds to offset any reputational cost.

Managing Research as Competition Intensifies

U.S. firms that continue to support high-quality research have understood the importance of providing clients with research that is distinctive, value added, and increasingly proprietary. Bernstein has focused on detailed and independent reports on large-cap stocks ("Black Books"), Leerink Swann on analyzing health stocks with proprietary access to its network of industry experts, and Sidoti on small-cap stocks that are not covered by other firms. All have succeeded in building reputations for research expertise in a specific space. Many have sought to limit access to those clients based on commission revenues.

Finally, successful U.S. firms see research as a critical service that adds value to clients and generates resources for the firm, rather than as a cost center. Credit Suisse demonstrated the feasibility of building a profit and loss statement for research in a way that supports the firm's business model and facilitates evaluating the performance of the department, individual analysts, and specific customers. This allows the firm to identify how the research department is performing and which analysts merit additional resources. The example of Prudential here is very illustrative. In its push to build its research business, Prudential opted to hire star analysts away from other firms but then had no way of understanding how much support was needed to help those analysts continue to be successful or how to evaluate the financial impact of research. As a consequence, many star analysts underperformed, and the firm ended up overpaying them for their services.

Implications for Sell-Side Analysts

Individual analysts can benefit from an understanding of the recent trends in the U.S. equity research market. First, it is critical to manage one's franchise like a business: provide value-added products and services to clients that they are willing to pay for, even when growth slows and budgets inevitably come under pressure. Providing a differentiated product is one way to achieve this goal—covering smaller-cap stocks that receive little to no research attention, covering well-followed companies or industries in a unique way, or doing proprietary field research.

Second, analysts should recognize and utilize the platforms their firms provide them. Investment firms differ in their research capabilities and platforms. Research has shown that analysts who move between firms often see a decline in their performance. With turnover of the best and brightest on the rise, analysts should consider this potential downside before switching firms.[1]

Third, clients increasingly value coordinated research efforts—research that crosses geographic borders, industry groups, and asset classes. Collaborating with colleagues to provide this type of research product is a key way to add value from a client's perspective—one for which they are willing to pay. However, many analysts think of themselves as individual free agents. Having collaboration skills is becoming more and more important in a globally interconnected economy.

Finally, analysts need to manage their careers strategically and be on the lookout for new trends and ideas. Equity analysts need to acquire an understanding of global and fixed income markets and to develop a skill set and knowledge base that allow them to provide value to a diverse set of customers, including hedge funds as well as traditional institutions.

Implications for Buy-Side Firms

Buy-side analysts and firms can also benefit from reflecting on the recent trends that have characterized the sell-side industry.

First, buy-side firms can adopt some of the performance measurement and management tools employed by the sell-side industry. The sell side has developed significantly more advanced measurement metrics that allow managers to identify and reward high performers and to manage out those analysts who are not performing well.

Second, buy-side firms would do well to provide opportunities for their analysts to discuss and debate their investment ideas. Sell-side analysts spend a considerable amount of time discussing their ideas with buy-side clients and coverage company management teams. These conversations help to shape their ideas and strengthen their arguments. Buy-side firms should create forums, such as investment committees and informal research meetings, that provide their own analysts with opportunities to discuss and debate their ideas and investment theses with multiple parties to ensure that the logic and arguments underlying these ideas are solid.

Third, buy-side firms can develop a better model for how their analysts add value relative to sell-side peers. There is little to no benefit in recreating what the sell side does—that approach would create zero value for the buy-side firm. Instead, buy-side analysts should focus on developing proprietary research ideas and spend time on other differentiated analyses.

Finally, while buy-side analysts do not face the same, or perhaps as many, conflicts as their sell-side peers, they do face conflicts. One such conflict emerges from their relationships with portfolio managers, who have the ultimate decision-making power over an analyst's ideas and often have greater status within the firm. According to buy-side analysts, portfolio managers' existing stock holdings have potential to create ineffective dynamics in analyzing these stocks. Portfolio managers also have access to the same sell-side resources and can be reluctant to listen to their analysts' ideas. It is important for buy-side firm managers to manage these conflicts to ensure that their internal research resources are being effectively utilized.

We conclude this book on a note of optimism. Despite its many recent challenges, the sell-side research industry has time and again demonstrated the ability to reposition itself for success. Given the importance of reliable information for the effective functioning of financial markets, the industry continues to meet a fundamental investor need. Admittedly, technology has enabled other information providers to compete with analysts in serving this role. But technology also generates new opportunities for sell-side analysts to undertake proprietary research. The emergence of new rapidly growing markets also poses a remarkable opportunity for the industry. Given these changes and the dynamism of financial markets, what will surely be true is that the industry will continue to evolve.

Reference Matter

Notes

Preface

1. The book draws on the following articles and cases: Amanda Paige Cowen, Boris Groysberg, and Paul Healy, "Which Types of Analyst Firms Are More Optimistic?" *Journal of Accounting & Economics*, volume 41, numbers 1–2 (April 2006), pp. 119–146; Boris Groysberg, Linda-Eling Lee, and Ashish Nanda, "Can They Take It with Them? The Portability of Star Knowledge Workers' Performance: Myth or Reality," *Management Science*, volume 54 (July 2008), pp. 1213–1230; Boris Groysberg, Paul M. Healy, and David A. Maber, "What Drives Sell-Side Analyst Compensation at High-Status Investment Banks?" *Journal of Accounting Research*, volume 49 (2011), pp. 969–1000; Boris Groysberg, Paul Healy, Nitin Nohria, and George Serafeim, "What Factors Drive Analyst Forecasts?" *Financial Analysts Journal*, volume 67, number 4 (July–August 2011), pp. 18–29; Boris Groysberg, Paul Healy, George Serafeim, and Devin Shanthikumar. "The Stock Selection and Performance of Buy-Side Analysts." *Management Science* (forthcoming); David Maber, Boris Groysberg, and Paul Healy, "How Do Sell-Side Analysts Communicate with Their Client Investors?" Working paper, September 2012, Harvard Business School; Ashish Nanda and Boris Groysberg, "Lehman Brothers (C): Decline of the Equity Research Department," HBS No. 902-003 (Boston: Harvard Business School Publishing, 2001); Boris Groysberg, Paul M. Healy, and Amanda Cowen, "Prudential Securities," HBS No. 104-008 (Boston: Harvard Business School Publishing, 2004); Boris Groysberg and Anahita Hashemi, "Sanford C. Bernstein: Growing Pains," HBS No. 405-011 (Boston: Harvard Business School Publishing, 2004); Ashish Nanda, Boris Groysberg, and Lauren Prusiner, "Lehman Brothers (A): Rise of the Equity Research Department," HBS No. 906-034 (Boston: Harvard Business School Publishing, 2006); Boris Groysberg and Ashish Nanda, "Lehman Brothers (D): Reemergence of the Equity Research Department," HBS No. 406-090 (Boston: Harvard Business School Publishing, 2006); Boris Groysberg and Andrew N. McLean, "Leerink Swann & Co.: Creating Competitive Advantage," HBS No. 406-060 (Boston: Harvard Business School Publishing, 2006); Boris Groysberg and Ingrid Vargas, "Innovation and Collaboration at Merrill Lynch," HBS No. 406-081 (Boston: Harvard Business School Publishing, 2008); Boris Groysberg, Victoria W. Winston, and Robin Abrahams, "Teena Lerner: Dividing the Pie at Rx Capital (A)," HBS No. 409-058 (Boston: Harvard Business School Publishing, 2008); Boris Groysberg, Paul M. Healy, and Sarah Abbott, "Credit Suisse Group: Managing Equity Research as a Business," HBS No. 410-073 (Boston: Harvard Business School Publishing, 2010); Boris Groysberg, Paul M. Healy, and Sarah Abbott, "Sidoti & Company: Launching a Micro-Cap Product," HBS No. 411-072 (Boston: Harvard Business School Publishing, 2011); Boris Groysberg, Paul M. Healy, and Sarah Abbott. "Morgan Asset Management." HBS No. 411-058 (Boston: Harvard Business School Publishing, 2011); and Boris Groysberg, Paul M. Healy, and Sarah Abbott, "Gerson Lehrman Group: Managing Risks," HBS No. 412-004 (Boston: Harvard Business School Publishing, 2012).

In addition, we have conducted more than 100 interviews, which provide us with rich qualitative data from the field that reveals many of the relationships that we found in academic papers, as well as six in-depth studies of research providers that are following different types of models and strategies.

Chapter 1

1. The Prudential Insurance Company, *The Power of a Story* (New York: Harcourt Inc., 2001), pp. 49–51.

2. "Prudential Offers $385 Million for Bache," *Dow Jones Newswires*, March 19, 1981, via Factiva.

3. Jessica Sommar, "Rock Slide," *Investment Dealers' Digest*, April 1, 1991, pp. 20–27.

4. Ibid., p. 21.

5. Ibid., p. 22.

6. Ibid., p. 22.

7. Ibid., pp. 21–24.

8. Ibid., p. 24.

9. Ibid., p. 25.

10. Suzanna Andrews, "The Strange, Charmed Life of Wick Simmons," *Institutional Investor*, January 1, 1995, *via* Factiva.

11. Jon Birger, "The Rock Is on a Roll: Prudential Wins Back Investment Business," *Crain's New York Business*, October 27, 1997, via Factiva.

12. Chris Clair, "Hedge Funds Drive Changes in Equity Trading," *HedgeWorld News*, August 27, 2007. Retrieved in April 2008 via Factiva; Jessica Papini, "Sell-Side Research Market Share to Plummet," *Wall Street Letter*, January 6, 2006; Greenwich Associates, "Commission Rates and Concentration of Business," 1977–2002.

13. Arden Dale, "US Equity Brokers' Commissions Still Feeling the Pinch," *Dow Jones Newswires*, June 28, 2006.

14. Jeff Franklin, "Brokers on the Bubble in Pru-Wachovia Deal: Only Top Producers to Be Offered Incentives to Stay," *Investment News*, March 3, 2003, via Factiva, retrieved on February 8, 2008.

15. "Wachovia Corp. and Prudential Financial, Inc. to Form Premier National Retail Financial Advisory Firm," *PR Newswire*, February 19, 2003, via Factiva, retrieved on February 8, 2008.

16. Ibid.

17. Glen Fest, "Going with the Flow," *US Banker*, April 1, 2003, via Factiva, retrieved on February 8, 2008.

18. Ibid.

19. Sam Ali, "Ex-Pru Staffer Charged by SEC," *Star Ledger*, November 5, 2003, via Factiva, retrieved on August 3, 2007.

20. Ibid.

Chapter 2

1. Michael Mayo, *Exile on Wall Street: One Analyst's Fight to Save the Big Banks from Themselves* (Hoboken, NJ: John Wiley & Sons, 2012).

2. Danielle Sessa, "All-Star Analysts 1999 Survey: Early Mornings, Late Nights Mark an Analyst's Days," *The Wall Street Journal*, June 29, 1999, p. R13.

3. Dan Reingold with Jennifer Reingold, *Confessions of a Wall Street Analyst* (New York: HarperCollins Publishers, 2006), p. 72.

4. N. R. Kleinfield, "The Many Faces of the Wall Street Analyst," *The New York Times*, October 27, 1985, via Factiva, retrieved in October 2008.

5. Boris Groysberg and Anahita Hashemi, "Sanford C. Bernstein: Growing Pains," HBS No. 405-011 (Boston: Harvard Business School Publishing, 2004), p. 13.

6. Ibid., p. 5.

7. Prior to 2002, Merrill Lynch recommendations also included a long-term investment recommendation.

8. Ashish Nanda, Boris Groysberg, and Lauren Prusiner, "Lehman Brothers (A): Rise of the Equity Research Department," HBS No. 906-034 (Boston: Harvard Business School Publishing, 2006), pp. 5–6.

9. Boris Groysberg, Paul Healy, Nitin Nohria, and George Serafeim, "What Factors Drive Analyst Forecasts?" *Financial Analysts Journal*, volume 67, number 4 (July–August 2011).

10. Jerry Borrell, "The Research Analyst," *Upside*, June 2002, via ABI/Inform Global.

11. Boris Groysberg and Ingrid Vargas, "Innovation and Collaboration at Merrill Lynch," HBS No. 406-081 (Boston: Harvard Business School Publishing, 2006), p. 19.

12. David Maber, Boris Groysberg, and Paul Healy, "How Do Sell-Side Analysts Communicate with Their Client Investors?" Working paper, September 2012, Harvard Business School.

13. Ibid.

14. Reingold, p. 43.

15. Peter Elkind, Mary Danehy, Jessica Sung, and Julie Schlosser, "Where Mary Meeker Went Wrong. She May Be the Greatest Dealmaker Around. The Problem Is, She's Supposed to Be an Analyst," *Fortune*, May 14, 2001, via Factiva, November 2008.

16. Peter Elkind Reporter Associates Mary Danehy, Jessica Sung, and Julie Schlosser, "Where Mary Meeker Went Wrong. She May Be the Greatest Dealmaker Around. The Problem Is, She's Supposed to Be an Analyst," *Fortune*, May 14, 2001, via Factiva, November 2008.

17. The term *Chinese walls* refers to the communication barriers that prevent investment bankers, who often possess material, nonpublic information about companies, from sharing that information with research analysts. These Chinese walls are strictly enforced, and analysts who receive nonpublic information are said to have been "brought over the wall." Once "over the wall" with regard to a company under coverage, an analyst is extremely limited in his or her ability to write about or comment on a company.

18. Justin Fox, "Why So Short Sighted?" *Fortune*, April 13, 2006, retrieved in September 2012 from http://money.cnn.com/magazines/fortune/fortune_archive/2006/04/17/8374283/index.htm.

19. Groysberg and Hashemi, p. 14.

20. Ibid., p. 17.

21. Boris Groysberg and Andrew N. McLean, "Leerink Swann & Co.: Creating Competitive Advantage," HBS No. 406-060 (Boston: Harvard Business School Publishing, 2004), p. 2.

22. Lydia Chavez, "The Making of a Securities Analyst," *The New York Times*, January 31, 1982, via Factiva, retrieved in November 2008.

23. Boris Groysberg, Paul M. Healy, and Sarah Abbott, "Credit Suisse Group: Managing Equity Research as a Business," HBS No. 410-073 (Boston: Harvard Business School Publishing, 2005), p. 1.

24. Boris Groysberg and Ingrid Vargas, "Innovation and Collaboration at Merrill Lynch," HBS No. 406-081 (Boston: Harvard Business School Publishing, 2005), p. 4.

25. Boris Groysberg and Ashish Nanda, "Lehman Brothers (D): Reemergence of the Equity Research Department," HBS No. 406-090 (Boston: Harvard Business School Publishing, 2006), p. 8.

26. Boris Groysberg, Linda-Eling Lee, and Ashish Nanda, "Can They Take It with Them? The Portability of Star Knowledge Workers' Performance: Myth or Reality," *Management Science*, volume 54 (July 2008), pp. 1213–1230.

27. Ashish Nanda, Boris Groysberg, and Lauren Prusiner, "Lehman Brothers (A): Rise of the Equity Research Department," HBS No. 906-034 (Boston: Harvard Business School Publishing, 2006), p. 10.

28. Groysberg and Hashemi, p. 11.

29. Ibid., p. 13.

30. Ibid, p. 13.

31. Groysberg and Nanda, p. 9.

32. Reingold, p. 34.

33. Nanda, Groysberg, and Prusiner, p. 6.

34. Boris Groysberg, Paul M. Healy, and David A. Maber, "What Drives Sell-Side Analyst Compensation at High-Status Investment Banks?" *Journal of Accounting Research*, volume 49 (2011), pp. 969–1000, and the HBS working paper with the same name.

35. Ibid., pp. 969–1000.

36. Ibid., pp. 969–1000.

37. Reingold, p. 186.

38. Groysberg, Healy, and Maber, pp. 969–1000.

Chapter 3

1. "Murray Safanie Is Dead at 68," *The New York Times*, January 14, 1968, ProQuest Historical Newspapers, retrieved in May 2008 from www.proquest.com.

2. Justin Schack, "The Pioneers," *Institutional Investor* (October 2001), p. 104.

3. Ibid.

4. "How Should Analysts Spend Their Time?" *Institutional Investor* (October 1967): pp. 20–24.

5. Ibid.

6. Boris Groysberg and Anahita Hashemi, "Sanford C. Bernstein: Growing Pains," HBS No. 9-405-011 (Boston, Harvard Business School Publishing, 2004).

7. Joe Kolman, "James Balog, Vice Chairman Drexel Burnham Lambert," *Institutional Investor* (June 1987), p. 233.

8. Phyllis Feinberg, "Hard-Dollar Research Gets the Hard Sell," *Institutional Investor*, November 1978, pp. 67–68.

9. N. R. Kleinfield, "The Many Faces of the Wall Street Analyst," *The New York Times*, October 27, 1985, via Factiva, retrieved on February 7, 2008.

10. Paul Strauss, "The Heyday Is Over for Analysts' Compensation," *Institutional Investor* (October 1977), pp. 121–211.

11. "The 1981 All-America Research Team," *Institutional Investor* (October 1981), pp. 49–55.

12. Ibid.

13. "The 1980 All-America Research Team," *Institutional Investor* (October 1980), pp. 39–44.

14. Ashish Nanda and Boris Groysberg, "Lehman Brothers (C): Decline of the Equity Research Department," HBS No. 902-003 (Boston: Harvard Business School Publishing, 2001), p. 2.

15. Joseph Nocera and Abrahm Lustgarten, "Wall Street on the Run," *Fortune*, June 14, 2004, via Factiva, retrieved in November 2008.

16. Nanda and Groysberg, p. 5.

17. *Nelson's Catalog of Institutional Research Reports*, 1999.

18. Jeffrey M. Laderman, "Wall Street's Spin Game," *Business Week*, October 5, 1998.

19. Ibid.

20. Ibid.

21. Boris Groysberg, Nitin Nohria, and Derek Haas, "1995 Release of the Institutional Investor Research Report: The Impact of New Information" HBS No. 408–061 (Boston: Harvard Business School Publishing, 2001).

22. "The 1998 All-American Research Team," *Institutional Investor* (October 1998), pp. 99–106.

23. Michael Siconolfi, "Shearson Research Analysts Finish First on 'All-America Team' for Third Year," *Wall Street Journal*, October 13, 1992.

Chapter 4

1. "Prudential Securities Launches New Investor-Focused Strategy," *Business Wire*, December 15, 2000, via Factiva, retrieved in November 2011.

2. Daniel Kadlec, "Buy! (I Need the Bonus); A Widening Probe of Stock Analysts Shows How They Have Long Played Average Investors for Chumps." *Time*, May 20, 2002, via Factiva, retrieved in January 2010.

3. Ibid.

4. Jeffrey M. Laderman, "Wall Street's Spin Game." *Business Week*, October 5, 1998.

5. Ellen E. Schultz, "Wall Street Grows Treacherous for Analysts Who Speak Out," *Wall Street Journal*, April 5, 1990.

6. Barbara Donnelly, "Tough Times for Research Directors." *Wall Street Journal*, May 28, 1991.

7. Michael Siconolfi and Anita Raghavan, "Brokers Launch Bidding War for Top Analysts," *Wall Street Journal*, August 4, 1995, via Factiva, retrieved on September 2012, 1995.

8. "Merrill Lynch Regains Conseco as a Customer as Analyst Departs," *The Wall Street Journal*, August 18, 1995, via Factiva, retrieved in August, 2012.

9. Jerry Knight, "'Marvin the Maven' vs. The Donald: How a Moment of Incite Cost an Analyst His Job," *The Washington Post*, April 3, 1990, via Factiva, retrieved in September 2012.

10. Debbie Galant, "The Hazards of Negative Research Reports," *Institutional Investor* (July 1990), p. 73.

11. Ibid.

12. Ibid.

13. Ibid.

14. Schultz.

15. Laderman.

16. Jon Birger, "Why Analysts Still Matter; They Are the Lowest of the Low, Right? Their Motives Are Suspect and Their Work Has No Real Value to Investors, Right? Wrong," *Money Magazine*, July 1, 2002, via Factiva, retrieved in November 2008.

17. Brooke Masters, "Downturn Hard to Bear for Bullish US Analysts," *Financial Times*, November 18, 2008, via Factiva, retrieved in November 2011.

18. Dan Reingold with Jennifer Reingold, *Confessions of a Wall Street Analyst* (New York: HarperCollins Publishers, 2006), p. 38.

19. John R. Dorfman, "1994 Was a Rough Year for Nation's Analysts," *The Tampa Tribune*, June 21, 1995, p. 7.

20. Laderman.

21. Affidavit in Support of Application for an Order Pursuant to General Business Law Section 354, filed in the case of In the matter of an inquiry by Eliot Spitzer, Attorney General of the State of New York, Petitioner, and Merrill Lynch & Co., et al., Respondents; Supreme Court of the State of New York, the Chief of the Investment Protection Bureau of the New York State Department of Law.

22. *Securities and Exchange Commission vs. Henry McKelvey Blodget*, U.S. District Court Southern District of New York, March 28, 2003, retrieved in September 2012 from www.sec.gov/litigation/complaints/comp18115b.htm.

23. NASD, "Letter of Acceptance, Waiver and Consent," NO. CAF030017, retrieved in September 2012 from www.finra.org/web/groups/industry/@ip/@enf/@da/documents/industry/p007669.pdf.

24. "Merrill Lynch Stock Rating System Found Biased by Undisclosed Conflicts of Interest," Office of the Attorney General, State of New York, April 8, 2002.

25. Hsiou-wei W. Lin and Maureen F. McNichols, "Underwriting Relationships, Analysts' Earnings Forecasts and Investment Recommendations," *Journal of Accounting and Economics*, volume 25, issue 1 (February 1998), pp. 101–127.

26. Patricia Dechow, Amy Hutton, and Richard Sloan, "The Relation between Analysts' Forecasts of Long-Term Earnings Growth and Stock Price Performance Following Equity Offerings," *Contemporary Accounting Research*, Spring 2000, pp. 1–32.

27. Hsiou–wei Lin, Maureen F. McNichols, and Patricia C. O'Brien, "Analyst Impartiality and Investment Banking Relationships," *Journal of Accounting Research*, volume 43, number 4 (2005): pp. 623–650.

28. Jay Ritter and Ivo Welch, "A Review of IPO Activity, Pricing and Allocations," Yale School of Management Working Papers, Yale School of Management, revised April 1, 2002.

29. David Denis and Mike Cliff, "How Do IPO Issuers Pay for Analyst Coverage?" *Journal of Investment Management*, volume 4 (2006), pp. 48–61.

30. The original ten firms were: Bear Stearns, Salomon Smith Barney, Credit Suisse, Goldman Sachs, Lehman Brothers, J. P. Morgan, Merrill Lynch, Morgan Stanley, Piper Jaffray, and UBS. Within a year of the original settlement, Thomas Weisel and Deutsche Bank came to terms with regulators.

31. This section draws from Addendum A of the Final Judgment for each firm. See "Additional Court Orders," retrieved on October 10, 2007, from www.globalresearchanalystsettlement.com/additional.php3.

32. U.S. Securities and Exchange Commission, "SEC Factsheet on Global Analyst Research Settlements," April 28, 2003; retrieved on September 18, 2007, from www.sec.gov/news/speech/factsheet.htm.

33. Credit Suisse Company Materials, February 2009.

34. The U.S. Equities Market Report, Institutional Investor Research Group, November 2003, p. 4.

35. TABB Group, "The Future of Equity Research: A 360o Perspective," June 29, 2006, in "US and UK Buy-side Firms' External Equity Research Spending to Fall from $7B in 2006 to $6B

in 2008 with Sell-Side Dropping 30% of Analysts, Says TABB Group Report on the Future of Equity Research," *Business Wire*, June 27, 2006, via Factiva; retrieved in February 2013.

36. Boris Groysberg and Ingrid Vargas, "Innovation and Collaboration at Merrill Lynch," HBS No. 406-081 (Boston: Harvard Business School Publishing, 2005), p. 3. Also, Mara Der Hovanesian and Amy Borrus, "Can the Street Make Research Pay? In the Eliot Spitzer Era, It's Looking More and More Like an Expensive Luxury," *Business Week*, January 31, 2005, via Factiva, retrieved in October 2008.

37. Der Hovanesian and Borrus.

38. *Department of Enforcement v. Jack Benjamin Grubman and Christine Ruzol Gochuico*, NASD Office of Hearing Officers, September 23, 2002, p. 5.

39. Christopher O'Leary, "Cracks in the Chinese Wall: Four Years after SEC Settlement, Is Street Research Withering in the Shadows?" *Investment Dealers Digest*, March 5, 2007, via Factiva, retrieved in August 2012.

40. "2007 All America Research Team," *Institutional Investor—Americas*, October 23, 2007.

41. Joseph A. Giannone, "Lifting the Lid—Wall St Research Suffers since Spitzer Deal," *Reuters News*, February 23, 2006, via Factiva, retrieved in August 2012.

42. "Unsettled on Wall Street," *Institutional Investor*, October 14, 2003, retrieved in August 2012 from www.institutionalinvestor.com/Popups/PrintArticle.aspx?ArticleID=1026784.

43. O'Leary.

44. Thomas D. Saler, "Rethinking Research," *Barrons*, January 22, 2007, via Factiva, retrieved in October 2008.

45. O'Leary, pp. 19–22.

46. Amanda Paige Cowen, Boris Groysberg, and Paul Healy. "Which Types of Analyst Firms Are More Optimistic?" *Journal of Accounting & Economics*, volume 41, numbers 1–2 (April 2006), pp. 119–146.

47. For example, CSFB reported only 110 client hits on independent research in the first Settlement year and only fifty-four in the second. Each of those hits cost roughly $100,000 ($10 million per year in independent research costs plus other implementation costs).

48. Greenwich Associates, Press Release, "U.S. Equity Research Providers: An End to the Brief Rise of Specialists and Independents? Citi Tops Greenwich Associates Equity Research Rankings in Market Share," July 22, 2008.

Chapter 5

1. Lynn Brenner, "The Bull and the Bear," *United States Banker* (January 1991).

2. Michael Mayo, *Exile on Wall Street: One Analyst's Fight to Save the Big Banks from Themselves* (Hoboken, NJ: John Wiley & Sons, 2012).

3. Michael Siconolfi, "Incredible 'Buys': Many Companies Press Analysts to Steer Clear of Negative Ratings—Stock Research Is Tainted as Naysayers Are Banned, Undermined and Berated—Small Investors in the Dark," *The Wall Street Journal*, July 19, 1995, via Factiva, retrieved in August 2012.

4. Matt Murray, "Sudden Departure of a Top-Rated Bank Analyst from Donaldson Lufkin Generates Questions," *The Wall Street Journal*, March 31, 1998, via Factiva, retrieved in August 2012.

5. Securities and Exchange Commission, 2000. Final Rule: Selective Disclosure and Insider Trading, Exchange Act Release No. 33-7881 Oct. 23. Available at www.sec.gov/rules/final/33-7881.htm.

6. Ibid.

7. Ibid.

8. Joseph Weber, "Full Disclosure for All," *Business Week*, September 16, 2000.

9. Brian Bushee, Dawn Matsumoto, and Greg Miller, "Open versus Closed Conference Calls: The Determinants and Effects of Broadening Access to Disclosure," *Journal of Accounting and Economics*, volume 34 (2003), pp. 149–180.

10. Andreas Gintschel and Stanimir Markov, "The Effectiveness of Regulation FD," *Journal of Accounting and Economics*, volume 37, issue 3 (September 2004), pp. 293–314.

11. P. S. Mohanram and S. Sunder, "How Has Regulation Fair Disclosure Affected the Operations of Financial Analysts?" *Contemporary Accounting Research*, volume 23, issue 2 (2006), pp. 491–525.

12. Karen Blumenthal, "Unseen Hands: Ever Wonder Who Calls Your Broker before Your Broker Calls You?" *National Post*, May 1, 2007.

13. Michael Mayo, "Accounting and Investor Protection Issues Raised by Enron and Other Public Companies," U.S. Senate Committee on Banking, Housing and Urban Affairs, March 19, 2002.

14. Justin Schack, "Capital Markets—So Much for the Little Guy," *Institutional Investor* (May 2007).

15. Eugene F. Soltes and David H. Solomon, "What Are We Meeting For? The Consequences of Private Meetings with Investors" Working Paper, Harvard Business School.

16. Eugene F. Soltes "Private Interaction between Firm Management and Sell-Side Analysts," Working Paper, Harvard Business School.

17. Business editors, "Nelson's Comprehensive, Worldwide Investment Research Database for Professional and Serious Investors Now Available on the Internet," *Business Wire*, February 17, 1998.

18. Eugene Grygo, "Brokers Help Buy-Side Firms Find Their Way in the Dark," *Financial News*, April 14, 2008, via Factiva, retrieved in September 2009.

19. The Lex Column, "Pressure on Research," *Financial Times*, September 7, 2007, via Factiva, retrieved in April 2009.

20. Josee Rose, "Brokers Commissions Drop as Electronic Trading Grows," *Dow Jones Newswires*, August 22, 2007, via Factiva, retrieved in April 2009.

21. Pierre Paulden, "TRADING—Daggers, Dark Pools and Disintermediation," *Institutional Investor—Americas*, April 12, 2007, via Factiva, retrieved in September 2009.

22. John D'Antona Jr., "Commissions Continue Spiral," *Traders Magazine*, July 1, 2012, via Factiva, retrieved in August 2012.

23. Greenwich Associates.

24. Paulden.

25. Jessica Papini, "Fido/Lehman Move May Squeeze Analyst Comp," *Wall Street Letter*, October 28, 2005, via Factiva, retrieved in September 2009.

Chapter 6

1. The recent growth in trading by hedge funds has increased demand for analysts to make sell recommendations as well as buys because hedge funds are looking for new short ideas.

2. Mark D'Avolio, "The Market for Borrowing Stock." *Journal of Financial Economics*, volume 66, issues 2–3 (November–December 2002), pp. 271–306, provides evidence on the costs of short-selling stock.

3. Soft dollars also create the risk for the bank that the client could find the research valuable but refuse to pay for it. However, this risk is reduced by the ongoing relationship between the bank and its client—if the client refuses to provide adequate reimbursement for past research, the bank can refuse to provide it with any future research.

4. Alexander Ljungqvist, Felicia Marston, Laura T. Starks, Kelsey D. Wei, and Hong Yan, "Conflicts of Interest in Sell-Side Research and the Moderating Role of Institutional Investors," *Journal of Financial Economics*, volume 85, issue 2 (August 2007), pp. 420–456.

5. Evidence by Malmendier and Shanthikumar suggests that small (retail) investors react naively to analyst recommendations and ignore their investment banking incentives, whereas large (institutional) investors discount analyst incentives appropriately (Ulrike Malmendier and Devin Shanthikumar, "Are Investors Naive about Incentives?" NBER Working Papers 10812 [2004], National Bureau of Economic Research, Inc.).

6. A full description of the study can be found in Amanda Paige Cowen, Boris Groysberg, and Paul Healy, "Which Types of Analyst Firms Are More Optimistic?" *Journal of Accounting & Economics*, volume 41, numbers 1–2 (April 2006), pp. 119–146.

7. Full-service banks also provide money management services to clients and use fees from this business to fund research, which creates another potential conflict of interest. Analysts interviewed at several banks noted that they face pressure to make optimistic forecasts and recommendations on a stock that is held by bank's money managers. This chapter does not examine this potential conflict.

8. Ernest Bloch, *Inside Investment Banking* (Washington, DC: Beard Books, 1989).

9. For our sample firm, at the end of 2004, less than 10 percent of the portfolio managers had been hired from its research department. Many of these had been with the company for twenty to thirty years.

10. In late 2004, StarMine Corp., a firm that analyzes and reports on the performance of member companies' financial analysts, began attracting buy-side clients. The sample firm signed up for StarMine after our study.

11. Many sell-side firms issued recommendations for only limited subperiods and therefore did not have sufficient data to enable us to compute meaningful return performance. Restricting sell-side firms to those that consistently issued recommendations ensured greater comparability between the buy- and sell-side firms in terms of the time period covered.

12. B. Barber, R. Lehavy, M. McNichols, and B. Trueman, "Buys, Holds, and Sells: The Distribution of Investment Banks' Stock Ratings and the Implications for the Profitability of Analysts' Recommendations," *Journal of Accounting and Economics*, volume 41, numbers 1–2 (2006), pp. 87–117.

13. Prior research (for example, Womack, 1996) indicates that sell-side analysts' recommendation updates affect returns when they are announced. Such is not likely to be the case for private buy-side recommendations. By excluding the returns on the date of the recommendation report, our tests therefore understate the relative profitability of sell-side recommendations. (Kent L. Womack, "Do Brokerage Analysts' Recommendations Have Investment Value?" *Journal of Finance*, volume 51, number 1 [March 1996]). We also computed returns to buying and holding stocks analysts at a firm rated as strong buy, buy or hold and shorting stocks rated as underperform or sell. Performance for both buy- and sell-side firms was weaker using this approach.

Chapter 7

1. Shubh Saumya, Jai Sinha, and Sudhir Jain, "Saving Sell-Side Research," Booz Allen Hamilton, 2006; available at www.boozallen.com/media/file/Saving_Sell-Side_Research.pdf.

2. Material included in this section is derived largely from Boris Groysberg, Paul M. Healy, and Sarah Abbott. "Morgan Asset Management," HBS No. 411-058 (Boston: Harvard Business School Publishing, 2011).

3. Ibid., p. 6.

4. Ibid.

5. Ibid.

6. Boris Groysberg, Victoria W. Winston, and Robin Abrahams, "Teena Lerner: Dividing the Pie at Rx Capital (A)," HBS No. 406-088 (Boston: Harvard Business School Publishing, 2006), p. 10.

7. Greenwich Associates.

8. Material included in this section is derived largely from Boris Groysberg and Ingrid Vargas, "Innovation and Collaboration at Merrill Lynch," HBS No. 406-081 (Boston: Harvard Business School Publishing, 2008).

9. Ibid., p. 9.

10. Ibid., p. 14.

11. Company website, Global Research: Products and Reports, retrieved in August 2010 from www.ml.com/index.asp?id=7695_8137_47928#GRH.

12. Material included in this section is derived largely from Boris Groysberg, Paul M. Healy, and Sarah Abbott. "Credit Suisse Group: Managing Equity Research as a Business." HBS No. 410-073 (Boston: Harvard Business School Publishing, 2010).

13. "Commissions: A Comparative Study" (New York: Institutional Investor Research Group, Institutional Investor Inc., 2004), p. 3.

14. Greenwich Associates.

15. Boris Groysberg, Paul M. Healy, and Sarah Abbott, "Credit Suisse Group: Managing Equity Research as a Business," HBS no. 410-073 (Boston: Harvard Business School Publishing, 2010), p.4.

16. Ibid.

17. Ibid., p. 5.

18. Ibid., p. 6.

19. Ibid., p. 8.

20. Material included in this section is derived largely from Boris Groysberg and Anahita Hashemi, "Sanford C. Bernstein: Growing Pains," HBS No. 405-011 (Boston: Harvard Business School Publishing, 2004), p. 9.

21. Ibid., pp. 4–5.

22. Ibid., p. 6.

23. Ibid., p. 9.

24. Ibid., p. 12.

25. Ibid., p. 12.

26. Material included in this section is derived largely from Boris Groysberg, Paul M. Healy, and Sarah Abbott, "Sidoti & Company: Launching a Micro-Cap Product," HBS No. 411-072 (Boston: Harvard Business School Publishing, 2011).

27. "Sidoti & Company Solidifies Its Leadership of the Micro-Cap Arena," PR Newswire, July 24, 2012, retrieved in August 2012 from www.prnewswire.com/news-releases/sidoti--company -solidifies-its-leadership-of-the-micro-cap-arena-163548296.html.

28. "The Competition"; retrieved in August 2012 from www.sidoti.com/aboutus/ thecompetition.aspx.

29. Groysberg, Healy, and Abbott, p. 3.

30. Groysberg, Healy, and Abbott, p. 5.

31. Groysberg, Healy, and Abbott, p. 4.

32. Sidoti analysts will not initiate coverage on a stock that is trading more than 10 percent below the analyst's price target.

33. Commission sharing agreements (CSAs) commonly known as "soft dollars" refer to the use of trade commissions to compensate third-party firms for research services provided. A buy-side client will execute a trade with a bulge-bracket firm but earmark a portion of the commission to be paid to a third-party firm as compensation for research services provided.

34. Material included in this section is derived largely from Boris Groysberg and Andrew N. McLean, "Leerink Swann & Co.: Creating Competitive Advantage," HBS No. 406-060 (Boston: Harvard Business School Publishing, 2006).

35. Boris Groysberg and Andrew N. McLean, "Leerink Swann & Co.: Creating Competitive Advantage," HBS No. 406-060 (Boston: Harvard Business School Publishing, 2006), p. 2.

36. Ibid., p. 2.

37. Ibid., p. 6.

38. Ibid., p. 4.

39. Material included in this section is derived largely from Boris Groysberg, Paul M. Healy, and Sarah Abbott, "Gerson Lehrman Group: Managing Risks," HBS No. 412-004 (Boston: Harvard Business School Publishing, 2012).

40. GLG's primary competitors included Guidepoint/Vista, with 130,000 experts covering technology, media, telecommunications, energy, industrials, retail, financial services, and leisure and gaming; Leerink Swann's MEDACorp, a network of 30,000 health care professionals; and Sermo, an online community of over 100,000 physicians.

41. Groysberg, Healy, and Abbott, "Gerson Lehrman Group," p. 5.

Chapter 8

1. Doug Cameron, "Prudential Securities Targets Europe and Latin America," *Financial Times*, March 15, 2001, via Factiva, retrieved in November 2011.

2. Seeking Alpha, December 13, 2009, retrieved in July 2011 from http://seekingalpha.com/ article/177932-household-savings-in-china-india-and-south-korea.

3. Reuters, "Chinese Investors Shrug off US Accounting Scandal," June 13, 2011, retrieved in July 2011 from www.cnbc.com/id/43376557.

4. "The Perils of Progress: As China's Financial System Liberalizes, What Will Become of Hong Kong?" *China Economic Review*, June 1, 2001, via Factiva, retrieved in July 2011.

5. "China PBOC Adviser Li Urges Savings Shift to Stocks," *Business Week*, December 1, 2010, re-trieved in July 2011 from www.businessweek.com/news/2010-12-01/china-pboc-adviser-li-urges -savings-shift-to-stocks.html.

6. "The Perils of Progress."

7. Shanghai Exchange, retrieved in June 2011 from http://edu.sse.com.cn/sseportal/en/home/ home.shtml, and Hong Kong Exchange, retrieved in June 2011 from http://www.hkex.com.hk/eng/ index.htm.

8. OneSource Information Services, Inc., retrieved in July 2011.

9. Freedom of the Press 2011 Survey Release, May 2, 2011, retrieved in June 2011 from www .freedomhouse.org/report/freedom-press/freedom-press-2011.

10. Reuters, "Chinese Investors Shrug off US Accounting Scandal."

11. Seeking Alpha, December 13, 2009.

12. Mythil Bhusnumath, "Savings Deposit: Last Frontier," *The Economic Times*, December 6, 2010, retrieved in July 2011 from http://articles.economictimes.indiatimes.com/2010-12-06/news/27620424_1_savings-rate-savings-bank-household-sector.

13. Securities and Exchange Board of India, *Annual Report 2009–10*, June 3, 2010, retrieved in July 2011 from www.sebi.gov.in/annualreport/0910/annualrep0910.pdf.

14. "Not a Retail Market; The Interesting Discovery, if You Trawl through the Disclosures on . . . ," *Business Standard*, June 9, 2011, via Factiva, retrieved in July 2011.

15. Handbook of Statistics on the Indian Securities Market 2010, SEBI, retrieved in July 2011 from www.sebi.gov.in/investor/handbook2010.pdf.

16. Freedom of the Press 2011 Survey Release.

17. Credit Suisse, "Research Strategic Initiatives," Research On-site—February 2011, p. 3.

18. Source: Capital IQ.

19. Nisha Gopalan, "WSJ Stockbrokers to Flock to Asia in Their Search for Growth," *Dow Jones Chinese Financial Wire*, November 30, 2010, via Factiva, retrieved in January 2011.

20. Ibid.

21. "Shanghai Stock Exchange," *The Handbook of World Stock, Derivative & Commodity Exchanges*, June 6, 2011, via Factiva, retrieved in July 2011.

22. *Institutional Investor, The 2010 All-America Research Team*, October 6, 2010, retrieved in January 2011 from www.institutionalinvestor.com/Research/961/What-Investors-Really-Want.html.

23. S&P "World by Numbers," in Richard Shaw, "Time to Change Country Mix in World Market-Cap," Seeking Alpha, June 22, 2008, retrieved in May 2011 from http://seekingalpha.com/article/82244-time-to-change-country-mix-in-world-market-cap.

Chapter 9

1. Boris Groysberg, Linda-Eling Lee, and Ashish Nanda, "Can They Take It with Them? The Portability of Star Knowledge Workers' Performance: Myth or Reality," *Management Science*, volume 54 (July 2008), pp. 1213–1230.

Index

Note: Page numbers in italic type indicate figures or tables.